HE LOVED THEM

Discovering Jesus' Heart for Seekers, Sinners,
Doubters, and the Discouraged
(and Other People Like Us)

JESSICA THOMPSON

MOODY PUBLISHERS

CHICAGO

Unless otherwise noted, all Scripture quotations are taken from the Christian Standard Bible®, Copyright © 2017 by Holman Bible Publishers. Used by permission. Christian Standard Bible® and CSB® are federally registered trademarks of Holman Bible Publishers.

Scripture quotations marked MSG are taken from THE MESSAGE, copyright © 1993, 2002, 2018 by Eugene H. Peterson. Used by permission of NavPress. All rights reserved. Represented by Tyndale House Publishers, a Division of Tyndale House Ministries.

Scripture quotations marked (NIV) are taken from the Holy Bible, New International Version®, NIV®. Copyright © 1973, 1978, 1984, 2011 by Biblica, Inc.™ Used by permission of Zondervan. All rights reserved worldwide. www.zondervan.com The "NIV" and "New International Version" are trademarks registered in the United States Patent and Trademark Office by Biblica, Inc.™

Scripture quotations marked NASB are taken from the New American Standard Bible® (NASB), Copyright © 1960, 1962, 1963, 1968, 1971, 1972, 1973, 1975, 1977, 1995, 2020 by The Lockman Foundation. Used by permission. www.Lockman.org

Scripture quotations marked (NLT) are taken from the Holy Bible, New Living Translation, copyright ©1996, 2004, 2015 by Tyndale House Foundation. Used by permission of Tyndale House Publishers, a Division of Tyndale House Ministries, Carol Stream, Illinois 60188. All rights reserved.

Edited by Annette LaPlaca
Interior design: Brandi Davis
Cover designer: Erik M. Peterson
Cover illustrations from the drawings of Rembrandt van Rijn (public domain)
Author photo: Jessica Delgado Photography

ISBN: 978-0-8024-2438-9

Originally delivered by fleets of horse-drawn wagons, the affordable paperbacks from D. L. Moody's publishing house resourced the church and served everyday people. Now, after more than 125 years of publishing and ministry, Moody Publishers' mission remains the same—even if our delivery systems have changed a bit. For more information on other books (and resources) created from a biblical perspective, go to www.moodypublishers.com or write to:

Moody Publishers
820 N. LaSalle Boulevard
Chicago, IL 60610

1 3 5 7 9 10 8 6 4 2

Printed in the United States of America

Praise for *He Loved Them*

This book does its job to overwhelm you with the love of Jesus. Every single chapter was Holy Spirit ministry. Jessica has a way of ushering her readers to look at Christ from a new perspective that engages the heart. I came away reading this book so encouraged, comforted, and restored. My soul needed it.

FINA OEI
Singer-songwriter and cofounder of Ladies Discipleship Ministry (LADIMI)

You won't be able to get through the first chapter without being in awe of how much Jesus loves you. Honestly, this book feels like the warmest, most welcoming hug in a prickly and hardened world we've been living in. Jess has a powerful way of helping us remember how tender Jesus is when we consistently fail. I love God so much more after reading this!

JAMI NATO
Author and entrepreneur

How we approach human beings portrayed in the Bible matters. Whenever we speak on biblical narratives, it is a retelling of another image bearer's story who is not here to fill in the details. It is easy to snatch a hot take from their stories without dipping a toe into their real human experience—the emotional, mental, social, cultural, and systemic nuances of it all. In *He Loved Them*, Jessica invites us to immerse ourselves into the humanity displayed in the gospel narratives—the complex, soil-soaked, screaming hot mess of life. She magnifies for us the posture of Christ's unashamed love for needy humans while spurring us on to love *and* action as Christ Himself displays—with tenderness, patience, and generosity. Anyone who feels inadequate or unseen in the trials of life will find solace in these pages. Anyone who struggles to see themselves in the gospel narratives will find their perspective broadened. Like your favorite gift-bearing auntie, Jessica guides readers through hard stories with wit and expertly placed superhero references, all the while wrapping the reader in kindness that leads to conviction, compassion, and comfort.

JENNIFER JI-HYE KO
Author of *A Lamenter's Pathway to Joy*

Every page of this read clarifies the good news of Jesus, that He is a Savior like no other. It will leave you feeling sought after, pursued, seen for who you are, and still loved. If you are needing a guide to help you remember that Jesus actually calls sinners to Himself, the run-down and wayward, this book will offer you hope.

HALEY MONTGOMERY
Musician, artist, author

To the burdened, the broken, the doubter,
the depressed, and the disillusioned.
May you find Jesus in these pages and see
that you were never lost to Him at all.

CONTENTS

LOVED THEM TO THE END

Having loved his own who were in the world, he loved them to the end.
JOHN 13:1

This is the God of the gospel of grace. A God who, out of love for us, sent
the only Son He ever had wrapped in our skin. He learned how to walk,
stumbled and fell, cried for His milk, sweated blood in the night,
was lashed with a whip and showered with spit, was fixed to a cross,
and died whispering forgiveness on us all.
BRENNAN MANNING

J esus "loved them to the end." He loved *us* to the end. His
heart has been and always will be a heart of love for His family. His heart has always been one that pursues and gathers and

redeems. The last words spoken by Christ on the cross reveal His heart toward His enemies: "Father, forgive them, because they do not know what they are doing." They reveal His heart toward the repentant recalcitrant: "Truly I tell you, today you will be with me in paradise." They reveal His heart toward His horrified friends and family: "Woman, here is your son" and "Here is your mother." They reveal the interworking of His heart and relationship with God the Father: "Father, into your hands I entrust my spirit." Jesus truly loved others until His last breath.

It's a heart-changing journey to spend time in God's Word looking purposefully at how Jesus loved and who He loved. Theoretically, I know Jesus loved, and I think you know that too. I expect we both believe Jesus was a loving and kind person, but I want to take you by the hand and show you the different and specific ways He loved and the types of people He loved.

My hope is that we all come away overwhelmed by the beauty of His love, overwhelmed by the beauty of His heart for myriads of people. Because we're studying Jesus, we will mostly be delving into the Gospels (Matthew, Mark, Luke, and John). With serious time focused only in the Gospels and reading them in several translations, we will immerse ourselves in the life of Christ. The different authors of each of the Gospels chose different aspects of Christ's life to emphasize depending on their values and what each wanted to convey to their particular audience. These episodes from Jesus' life, which show Him interacting with people of all kinds, will captivate you with the depth and the riches of Christ's love for sinners.

It's natural that we tend to think about Jesus' love for us. Our relationship with Jesus is so important to us that we don't tend to get past ourselves. We think, "Jesus loves *me*; now I am forgiven and my relationship with God is all good because of what Christ has done." Of course, that's all true, and we celebrate that truth. But who were the others Jesus loved as "His own"? Investigating the way Christ lived and loved can affect and change what we know about the world, God, each other, and ourselves.

As a starting point, we'll focus on Christ's humanity, taking a broad look at what His life meant. After that broad look, we will dive deeply into the personal interactions Jesus had with doubters and deniers, with those who were discouraged or in danger, with those in desperate need, and more. Though I hope you'll start with chapter 1, after that you can go ahead and "choose your own adventure." There's no rule that says you have to read all the chapters in order. Go to the table of contents to see if you identify with a certain group of people and skip right to that chapter. Skip around where your attention is drawn, and then finish with the last chapter.

As you investigate how Christ has interacted with the people in the categories you identify with, you will be amazed and drawn more deeply into His love and care for you. You may be reminded of times and events you wish you'd never had to experience, but looking back, you will find Jesus was always there. He is there no matter what type of person you are or what you have done or what has been done to you. Jesus is there, calling you and reminding you that the Father is coming toward you with arms opened wide.

While you're reading, resist the temptation to preach to yourself, "You ought to be more like Christ," or to despair with feelings that "I could never love the way He did!" Don't even admire from afar with, "That kind of love is so commendable." Instead, remember that Jesus is your righteousness. He's an example of love, but His perfect life and perfect love have become your own record of behavior before God. His righteousness is yours! You can focus freely on how Jesus has loved you personally. His love extends to and covers all your failures to love and hides you in His perfect love.

My prayer is that you'll finish reading with a heart enflamed by the fullness of Christ's love. Happy reading, dear friends.

one

JESUS, THE MOST COMPLETE HUMAN

You know that he was revealed so that he might take away sins,
and there is no sin in him.

1 JOHN 3:5

At the time of Jesus' coming the world was in a desperate situation. God had created the world with perfect *shalom* (completeness, wholeness, peace). Adam and Eve experienced this shalom with God—there was nothing that hindered their relationship with Him. They experienced shalom within themselves—no ego got in the way of honesty about who they were. They experienced shalom with each other—they didn't hide from each other or hurt each other; they enjoyed only love and community. Adam and Eve experienced shalom with creation—they didn't seek to dominate creation and use it for their own gain. They only sought to rule over it and subdue it as God had commanded them. But you know the story. They disobeyed God, and with that act of disobedience came broken shalom with God, within the self, with each other, and with creation. When Jesus entered the story, the people of the world were desperate for a way to restore shalom and to live the way they were meant to live.

Right into this dark and desperate world, the plan of redemption is enacted. God does what He always does: He takes the darkness and speaks light into it, creating something out of nothing. Jesus comes, heaven come to earth. As He brings heaven to earth, it changes everything for us. Romans 5:6 describes it: "For while we were still helpless, at the right time, Christ died for the ungodly."

The movie *Avengers: Endgame* has a scene near the end that gets me hyped every time I see it. If you haven't seen it, spoiler alert! I am about to tell what happens. In this scene, it appears that all hope is lost. Our heroes have battled valiantly, but the enemy, Thanos, has proved too strong for them. Thor, Captain America, and Iron Man together are no match for him. We look on helplessly as Captain America seems to accept his fate; he knows he won't win, but he will fight anyway. Just then, in the background, a portal opens up, and through that portal walks Black Panther, Shuri, and Okoye, and behind them an enormous army of Wakandan warriors. Right then—right in that moment—you know the tide has turned.

When all seems helpless and hopeless, our Redeemer makes His appearance.

You know our heroes will save the day and defeat Thanos and his army. Reinforcements showed up at just the right time. I remember watching this movie on opening night in the movie theater. The teenagers in front of me were crying and laughing. While I was a tad bit more reserved, my heart felt that same happiness.

But a movie high can't compare to the exponentially higher joy I feel when I think about Christ coming into our hopeless world to save us. So, when you hear "at the right time Christ died for the ungodly," you can almost see that portal open, with redemption breaking through the fall. When all seems helpless and hopeless, our Redeemer makes His appearance, and you know who is about to win.

JESUS RESTORES SHALOM WITH GOD

Jesus lived in complete peace with God. Romans 5:1 points to Jesus as the One who brings us peace with God: "Therefore, since we have been justified by faith, we have peace with God through our Lord Jesus Christ."

Looking back to the original status of things in the garden, we see Adam and Eve at complete peace with God. They walked and talked in the garden with Him. They were naked and unashamed

> If you feel a pull toward living at peace with God, it is because you were made for it! Your heart was made to find its satisfaction in Him.

before Him. What a beautiful picture. In their relationship there was no striving, no fear, no hiding. This is also the way Jesus lived in relationship to the Father.

Doesn't your heart long for that relationship of trust and rest? If you feel a pull toward living at peace with God, it is because you were made for it! Your heart was made to find its satisfaction in Him. Jesus knew this and modeled that life of peace with God to the fullest.

Jesus said He always lived to do the things that pleased the Father, not to gain or earn anything by it but because that was His greatest joy (John 8:29). Jesus always resisted temptation. Where Adam and Eve failed, Jesus succeeded. He lived at peace with God. Jesus lived out shalom. Christ's life of perfect peace with God was the key to undoing the effects of the fall. Jesus' life of complete shalom with God didn't just affect Him. The way Jesus lived affected all of creation from eternity past to eternity future.

Because of the way Jesus lived—because He lived as a perfect human was meant to live—we are now justified. His life of choosing to love and honor God, of being perfect, is now our record, given to us as a gift of grace. God sees us as perfect. We are hidden in Christ. His death to atone for all our sins makes us completely forgiven. Jesus' resurrection was the sign that God accepted His work on our behalf. We now have peace with God. Easter is the start of something; it is the launching of the new world. God will do for all of creation what He did for Jesus—providing rebirth, remaking, renewing. Redemption is for all of us, and we can take part in it. This peace that Jesus experienced with God was a peace for the world. Jesus, the Prince of Peace, didn't just sit back and relax; He actively worked to restore and give peace to others. His life brings the promise of peace on earth and good will to all people.

JESUS RESTORES SHALOM WITH SELF

Jesus knew who He was, and He lived fully in His identity of the Beloved. Jesus didn't try to be anything other than what He was. He never doubted who He was or what He was meant to do. We see this in the temple when Jesus was a young boy: "Didn't you know it was necessary for me to be in my Father's house?" (Luke 2:49), and it was clearly declared when He was baptized: "This is my beloved Son" (Matt. 3:17). Jesus embodied the perfect example of living at peace with self.

Peace with ourselves is also part of what God intended for us from the beginning. It's what we were created for: to know who we are without constant second-guessing or underlying feelings of inadequacy or feeling like unworthy impostors.

This shalom with self doesn't mean that Jesus didn't face any hardship or ask God for a different way to accomplish salvation, but He ultimately submitted to God's will. As He prayed in Gethsemane, Jesus petitioned for some other way to accomplish the plan of redemption, praying openly, vulnerable with His thoughts, not trying to sugarcoat His feelings. Jesus cried out to His Father. Jesus, who had always experienced complete and uninterrupted peace with His Father, was going to experience a divide—a break in relationship—for our sake. That is the thought that made Jesus sweat great drops of blood (Luke 22:44). Where Adam and Eve failed in the garden of Eden, Jesus prayed in the garden of Gethsemane that His Father's will be done. Jesus succeeded and won for us a new identity. He redeemed us to make us accepted and loved.

> Jesus won for us a new identity. He redeemed us to make us accepted and loved.

JESUS RESTORES SHALOM WITH OTHERS

Jesus lived to make peace with others. Matthew 9:36 says, "When he saw the crowds, he felt compassion for them, because they were distressed and dejected, like sheep without a shepherd." *The Message* puts it this way: "Then Jesus made a circuit of all the towns and villages. He taught in their meeting places, reported kingdom news, and healed their diseased bodies, healed their bruised and hurt lives. When he looked out over the crowds, his heart broke. So confused and aimless they were, like sheep with no shepherd."

Jesus did not consider equality with God a thing to be grasped but made Himself a servant (Phil. 2:6–7). He loved others, provided for them, healed them, and restored them. He looked for the marginalized and brought them in. His whole life was filled with service. He empathized with others, felt compassion, hurt with people. He wanted people to be whole; this was His mission. Jesus didn't just make them whole physically, but worked toward their wholeness emotionally and spiritually. He loved people into new life.

JESUS RESTORES SHALOM WITH CREATION

Jesus introduces a new way of living, one of giving instead of consuming. Colossians 1:19–20 says, "For God was pleased to have all his fullness dwell in him, and through him to reconcile everything to himself, whether things on earth or things in heaven, by making peace through his blood, shed on the cross."

What does the Bible say about how Jesus interacts with creation? You may not have considered this question very often, but it is essential to learning who Jesus is and how He experienced the wholeness of shalom. Jesus is reconciling creation to Himself. He sees the flowers of the field. Not a bird falls from the sky without His noticing. Jesus walked on water. He wasn't afraid of the storms while out at sea; He actually slept in the boat while the storm raged around Him. Lisa Sharon Harper, in her book *The Very Good Gospel*, writes,

> Jesus exercised dominion over creation to serve humanity. He multiplied bread and fish to feed thousands, and he smeared mud on the eyes of a blind man to give him sight (see John 9:1–12). Later Jesus was crucified on a tree. God—the Creator of the tree—was nailed to it. The original

sin of humanity was committed in relation to a tree, the Tree of the Knowledge of Good and Evil. Now the redemption of humanity and the reversal of the Fall happens in relation to a tree. Then Jesus conquered death, opening his own grave. And in the end there is only one tree, the Tree of Life. The tree's leaves are for the healing of the nations (see Revelation 22:1-2).[1]

Jesus lived in a way that redeemed and restored every part of creation. Because of what He has done, now we can partake in redemption; we can do this through our work and our vocation. We now are living into the holy mystery—this mystery that God uses His created ones, who were broken by the fall, to bring about His redemption. Because of the way He lived, we now experience in part that same restored shalom.

It is important to understand how the wholeness of Christ's life is pushing to bring heaven down to earth, pushing to reverse the effects of the fall. Together, let's look over Jesus' shoulder and see how Jesus lived in shalom, observing the way He loved. By the power of the Holy Spirit, we will seek to become more like Him. We will understand what it means to bring shalom to others and to live in shalom ourselves.

two

JESUS WITH
THE DOUBTERS

*The world of Christian faith is not a fairy-tale, make-believe world,
question-free and problem-proof, but a world where doubt is never far
from faith's shoulder.*

OS GUINNESS

*Then he said to Thomas, "Put your finger here; see my hands. Reach out
your hand and put it into my side. Stop doubting and believe." Thomas said
to him, "My Lord and my God!"*

JOHN 20:27–28 NIV

When Jesus was putting together His team of disciples, the
ones who would spend every day of His ministry life by
His side, supporting and helping Him, He put together the most

normal and average group of men and women you could imagine. Jesus included those with weak faith; He included the doubter. If I were to put together a support system, I would load it up with hype men and women. I'd want to look around and see a group of friends who believed in me more than I believed in myself.

Jesus didn't operate with a need for hype men; Jesus needed only the love of His Father. Jesus' sufficiency came from the perfect love shared between Father, Son, and Holy Spirit. That love within the triune Godhead was His operating system. That love enabled Him to deal so gently with those who doubted Him.

Three stories about Jesus encountering doubters provide a beautiful demonstration of Christ's love at work with those whose faith was weak. These people were believers. They came to Jesus. They wanted to be near Him. But they also doubted. Their hearts were conflicted.

A FAMILY OF DOUBTERS

Some of the doubters Jesus encountered were part of His own family. Matthew 12:46–50 tells the story:

> While Jesus was still talking to the crowd, his mother and brothers stood outside, wanting to speak to him. Someone told him, "Your mother and brothers are standing outside, wanting to speak to you." He replied to him, "Who is my mother, and who are my brothers?" Pointing to his disciples, he said, "Here are my mother and my brothers. For whoever does the will of my Father in heaven is my brother and sister and mother." (NIV)

This story appears just a few verses after Matthew recounts how the religious leaders were accusing Jesus of casting out demons by the power of the devil (Matt. 12:22–37). His mother and brothers undoubtedly heard about this; they knew all the rumors about Jesus. They were familiar with the way the religious leaders talked about Him, and they were worried. Something needed to be done, and they were going to do it. They were staging an intervention of sorts. Rumors were swirling about the things Jesus was doing and what He was saying. He had a strange group of people following Him and listening to all His teachings. And it was just Jesus—her son, their brother, the one they'd lived with day after day, eating meals, sharing a home. It was Jesus, who'd been a carpenter only a year ago—and now look at Him! Who did He think He was? So Jesus' family went to Him. They would remind Him of where He came from; they would bring Him home.

Even Mary—the one who was visited by an angel sent by God, conceived a baby without the help of any man, saw the shepherds come to praise her baby, received the gifts from the wise men, and heard Anna's and Elizabeth's prophetic words spoken over her son—knew better than anyone else about who this man Jesus was, and yet she doubted. She went to bring Him home; she went to rein Him in: "When his family heard about this, they went to take charge of him, for they said, 'He is out of his mind'" (Mark 3:21 NIV).

These family members send word to Jesus: "Your family is here. They want to talk with you." How does Jesus deal with this request? By redefining what family means. Jesus invites everyone in. The doubts of His mother and brothers do not make Him question His mission. Jesus reminds them and us that the way to be a part of the family is to remember who the true Father is and to live in that relationship.

> Jesus uses the doubt of His own family members to call more people to Himself.

Jesus uses the doubt of His own family members to call more people to Himself. His statement doesn't exclude His family, but rather continues to demonstrate to them the truth of who He is. Their doubt is the catalyst to bring more people into the family of God, to bring more people truly home. One commentator writes,

> Jesus was not so much concerned with traditional family arrangements as he was with the in-breaking of the Kingdom of God . . . and how this anticipation required a new kind of household. *Blood relatives and language were no longer decisive criteria for the new Household that God and the ministry of Jesus make possible.*[1]

YOU STILL DON'T KNOW ME?

Some of the closest friends of Jesus struggled to fully grasp who He was. The book of John gives us a glimpse of this in John 14:8–11, where Jesus responds to Philip's questions:

> "Lord," said Philip, "show us the Father, and that's enough for us." Jesus said to him, "Have I been among you all this time and you do not know me, Philip? The one who has seen me has seen the Father. How can you say, 'Show us the Father'? Don't you believe that I am in the Father and the Father is in me? The words I speak to you I do not speak on my own. The Father who lives in me does his works. Believe me that I am in the Father and the Father is in me. Otherwise, believe because of the works themselves."

This little interchange takes place near the end of Christ's ministry. Jesus is sitting with His disciples and preemptively comforting and preparing their hearts for what is about to happen. He tells those around Him, "I am the way, the truth, and the life. No one comes to the Father except through me. If you know me, you will also know my Father. From now on you do know him and have seen him" (John 14:6–7).

Jesus has just described Himself as the way to God, and Philip's response is to ask Jesus if they can just see God instead. Philip doesn't understand that Jesus has essentially explained to them that He and the Father are one. It's not just that Philip doesn't completely understand, but rather that He struggles to believe this claim. *How can Jesus and God be one? Is Jesus really claiming to be the Father? How is this even a possibility?*

Commentator Frederick Bruner explains what's happening in this exchange between Philip and Jesus: "The human being wants to know God. Jesus says, in effect, 'Welcome home.'"[2]

Jesus leans into Philip's doubts and one more time—for the millionth time—tells him, "I am the One you are looking for." Then Jesus tells Philip and the other disciples, who I am sure have the same questions and doubts as Philip, that He never does anything without His Father. Jesus explains that He only speaks the Father's words and only does what the Father wants. Jesus doesn't get angry at Philip for his question. He doesn't roll His eyes and walk away angry because, after months and months, these guys still don't get it. He just tells him again, "I'm the One."

Jesus makes a concession for Philip and essentially says, "If you can't believe I and the Father are locked together, then please just look at the things you have seen Me do and ask yourself, 'Who could do these things except for God Himself?'" Jesus basically says, "If you can't believe your ears, if you can't let your heart believe, then just go ahead and believe your eyes. You have seen the evidence. Believe what you have seen." Jesus appeals to the natural to prove the supernatural. He doesn't demand that Philip rise above and just believe. Jesus takes him back to all the things Philip had experienced and asks him to look, to remember, and to believe. He doesn't say, "I shouldn't have to prove Myself to you. You should just trust Me." Jesus builds Philip's faith. He does not shame Philip for his doubt.

MY LORD AND MY GOD!

Thomas may be the most well-known doubter from Scripture, and most of us are familiar with his story from John 20:24–29:

> Now Thomas [called "Twin"], one of the Twelve, was not with the disciples when Jesus came. So the other disciples told him, "We have seen the Lord!" But he said to them, "Unless I see the nail marks in his hands and put my finger where the nails were, and put my hand into his side, I will not believe." A week later his disciples were in the house again, and Thomas was with them. Though the doors were locked, Jesus came and stood among them and said, "Peace be with you!" Then he said to Thomas, "Put your finger here; see my hands. Reach out your hand and put it into my side. Stop doubting and believe." Thomas said to him, "My Lord and my God!" Then Jesus said, "Because you have seen me, you have believed; blessed are those who have not seen and yet have believed." (NIV)

This interchange between Thomas and Jesus takes place after Jesus' death and resurrection. Jesus has appeared to Mary at the tomb and then to most of His disciples. The other ten disciples tell Thomas that Jesus is alive, but Thomas remains skeptical: "I'll believe it when I see it." Then eight days later Jesus comes to him. Think of how Thomas felt during those eight days. Perhaps Thomas sat uncomfortably with his doubts and skepticism. Maybe he felt vindicated, having laid down an impossible ask, thrown the ultimate gauntlet.

But then Jesus comes. I love the scene being set in these verses. The disciples are indoors; the doors are locked. The disciples are probably still scared about what had happened, scared they would be uncovered as followers of Christ. They were uncertain about their future and perhaps even about their faith. And then Jesus appears! He greets His disciples with "Peace be with you." Then He turns His attention to Thomas, singling him out. He doesn't define Thomas by the doubts Thomas had, like we do. Jesus defines Thomas by His own great love for him. Jesus proves to be the Good Shepherd here, and He goes after Thomas, the struggling one. Jesus turns His gaze to him. Can you even imagine what must have been going through Thomas's mind? I mean, he'd been wrong—really wrong. I know when I am wrong about something or someone, I fully expect to be called out over it. I don't expect grace or kindness. I expect justice. But that's not the way of our Savior. Jesus says, "Look. Touch. See. Don't be faithless but believe." And Thomas responds with, "My Lord and my God!" My Lord and my God. Jesus claims Thomas as His, and Thomas responds by claiming Jesus as his.

Because Jesus cried out "My God, my God, why have you forsaken me" (NIV), Thomas was able to cry out "My Lord and my God!" and be completely accepted. The *Africa Bible Commentary* describes the way Jesus responds to our doubts:

> On such occasions Jesus stands like a mother beside us to protect us. In our fears, our confusion, our anxiety and our

> **Jesus doesn't define Thomas by his doubts. Jesus defines Thomas by His own great love for him.**

sinfulness, the risen Lord stands with his own and among his own. Like a mother Jesus takes us into his arms to protect us. When Jesus is with us, we know that we are blessed with the peace of his presence. Today our world is cruel and often frightening. We are fearful and prefer to stay behind closed doors. At such moments Jesus Christ comes to us, without being invited, and takes the central place by calming the storms and declaring, *Peace be with you.*"[3]

In the midst of our doubts, we can be completely honest with God about them. Beloved, Jesus didn't define His own family or Philip or Thomas by their doubts. Jesus doesn't define you by yours either; He defines you as His dearly loved child. He comes in patience. He comes in kindness. He comes to us right where we are so we can then fall back in amazement at His love and say, "My Lord and my God!" If you are doubting today, He is patient with your doubt. Remember these stories. Remember the kindness and love of Jesus. Pray for the faith to cry out "My Lord and my God!" Jesus has a word for you as well: "Blessed are those who have not seen me and yet believe."

If you are doubting today, He is patient with your doubt.

Doubting one, you are blessed—truly blessed. Jesus understands how difficult it would be to believe and not see. Because of that He proclaims a blessing over you if you do believe, even if your faith is weak—maybe especially if your faith is weak.

three

JESUS WITH THE DISCOURAGED

The Gospels suggest that when we watch Jesus, we are watching God love us.
PAUL MILLER

Seeing the crowds, He felt compassion for them, because they were distressed and downcast, like sheep without a shepherd.
MATTHEW 9:36 NASB

We have a God who shows up in the most unlikely places. His delight in surprising and caring for His children in unique ways is a wonder to behold.

Let's peer back in history to a dusty road that leads out of Jerusalem and into Emmaus. This same road leads out of discouragement and into hope renewed, and it leads from confusion to revelation. But before we make that turn toward hope and revelation, let's take a moment to consider the discouragement and confusion.

> Now that same day two of them were on their way to a village called Emmaus, which was about seven miles from Jerusalem. Together they were discussing everything that had taken place. And while they were discussing and arguing, Jesus himself came near and began to walk along with them. But they were prevented from recognizing him. Then he asked them, "What is this dispute that you're having with each other as you are walking?" And they stopped walking and *looked discouraged*. (Luke 24:13–17, emphasis added)

This story takes places after the death and—unbeknownst to these disciples—the resurrection of Christ. These two people are walking away from Jerusalem, where the unthinkable had just unfolded before them. They were disciples of Christ and had seen Him brutally murdered, and with that physical death their hope died as well. Sometimes because we are familiar with a story, we forget the humanity of those who lived it. Take a moment to think about how these two must have felt. Jesus was dead. The Roman empire (their physical oppressors) and the Pharisees (their spiritual oppressors) had exerted their ultimate power once again. The disciples left behind were confused, and they were arguing. *Hadn't Jesus just been celebrated and praised a week ago when He entered Jerusalem? Hadn't He only ever loved and served and helped? Hadn't Jesus explained the Scriptures in such a powerful way that He made them come alive? Why was He dead? Jesus was a good man!*

When Jesus comes to them on the road to Emmaus, He asks them a question. He comes near to hear what they have to say. "What is this dispute you are having with each other while you are walking?" He asks. They stop moving forward and look "discouraged." The Greek word used in this verse for *discouraged* literally means, "having a look suggestive of gloom or sadness, sad, gloomy, sullen, dark."[1] These Christ followers just flat out looked sad—so down and confused, and they didn't recognize that Jesus Himself was suddenly walking with them on this road.

These disciples are discouraged. Jesus comes to them, wanting to hear what they have to say. He draws near and wants to hear their hurt. Their pain and sadness don't repel Him.

The travelers are shocked by the question offered by the new arrival. In their upended world, the crucifixion of Jesus is the life-crushing event of their personal lives and the biggest news in Jerusalem. An equivalent might be someone dropping in on the evening of November 22, 1963 to ask, "What's the matter with everybody?" when the shock and horror of JFK's assassination had been so widely covered in the media and so all-encompassing in every American's day. To Cleopas and his fellow traveler, this question must have only deepened their sadness because they had to put words to all of their questions and doubts and broken dreams. "We were hoping that he was the one who was about to redeem Israel," they confide (Luke 24:21). There it was. The source of their discouragement. As Proverbs describes it, "Hope delayed makes the heart sick" (Prov. 13:12). Their hearts were sick.

Have you ever felt heartsick? Maybe you can't remember a time you *didn't* feel heartsick. I'm currently enduring a period of prolonged suffering. All the things I thought could never happen to me have happened, and now I'm saying things I never thought I would say about myself. I am divorced. I kept praying and hoping for a different outcome, but it hasn't happened and the end has come, and my heart is sick. Like the disciples, I am grieving a death of sorts that I never saw coming.

Jesus has this habit of showing up at the most unexpected times. After the travelers tell Him about their heartsickness, Jesus gives them some strong words: "How foolish you are, and how slow to believe all that the prophets have spoken! Wasn't it necessary for the Messiah to suffer these things and enter into his glory?" (Luke 24:25–26). After startling them with this direct challenge, Jesus then gives them God's Word: "Beginning with Moses and all the Prophets, he interpreted for them the things concerning himself in all the Scriptures" (v. 27). Jesus speaks directly to their sadness and points out their lack of belief. Jesus makes it clear—straight from the holy Scriptures—that what has happened is exactly what was supposed to happen! True to form, Jesus takes the time to do what He has just spent His years of ministry doing: teaching them. Jesus shows them how the death they are grieving is exactly what had to happen in order for Him to actually be what they had hoped for—the One to redeem Israel. He takes the time to show them that their hope wasn't misplaced at all.

The two disciples reach their final destination. They get where they were going, literally and figuratively. This was where Jesus wanted them. He wanted them to know that "hope delayed makes the heart sick, but desire fulfilled is a tree of life" (Prov. 13:12). When it looks as if their amazing new friend is going to move on and leave them, the travelers urge Him to come eat with them. They ask Him to stay. Jesus does, and then He opens their eyes not only to the reality of what had happened in Jerusalem but also to the reality of who He was:

Jesus did not ignore suffering. He spoke directly to it.

> It was as he reclined at the table with them that he took the bread, blessed and broke it, and gave it to them. Then their

eyes were opened, and they recognized him, but he disappeared from their sight. They said to each other, "Weren't our hearts burning within us while he was talking with us on the road and explaining the Scriptures to us?" (Luke 24:30–32)

These men had probably often eaten with the Savior, seeing Him bless and break bread. In this everyday pastime—sitting at a table and sharing a meal—Jesus reveals how near He is to those who are discouraged. He did not ignore the suffering of Cleopas and his companion. He spoke directly to it. He encouraged their hearts. He showed Himself to them.

And Jesus comes near to us. He wants us to believe wholeheartedly in the goodness of His character. He wants us to believe He will do what He says He will do, that He is who He says He is. Christ is our redemption, the One who will save us from our sins. Our hope is not misplaced. One Bible commentary explains it: "Here are two disciples who felt that the cross meant the end of the hope Jesus brought. Only Jesus himself, appearing in his restored existence, can change their minds. In every sense of the term, Jesus is the author of resurrection faith."[2]

When you feel as though your faith may be dead, Jesus comes to create life in your soul again. What these followers of Jesus thought was the end of all they had hoped for was just the beginning of more than they could ever have hoped to see accomplished.

DISTRESSED AND DEJECTED

I love how the Gospels give us a glimpse of Jesus' empathy for His people. Matthew 9:36 tells us, "When he saw the crowds, he felt compassion for them, because they were distressed and dejected, like sheep without a shepherd." *The Message* paraphrases this same passage:

Then Jesus made a circuit of all the towns and villages. He taught in their meeting places, reported kingdom news, and healed their diseased bodies, healed their bruised and hurt lives. When he looked out over the crowds, *his heart broke.* So confused and aimless they were, like sheep with no shepherd. "What a huge harvest!" he said to his disciples. "How few workers! On your knees and pray for harvest hands!" (Matt. 9:35–38 MSG, emphasis added)

After a long time spent healing those who needed healing and delivering those who needed deliverance, Jesus' loving heart is enflamed with compassion. He has seen His people hurting. "The vivid verb 'have compassion' (literally referring to a 'gut reaction') is always in the New Testament used of Jesus himself," writes R. T. France.[3] This *gut reaction* means Jesus can't help Himself. Because He is love, He must feel compassion when He sees suffering.

I have a few automatic responses myself. When I see one of my San Diego Padres (a major league baseball team that was so terrible for so long but is finally good...maybe? Hopefully!) hit a home run, I don't even think about my reaction. I automatically stand up, fists in the air, and start cheering. To be honest, I probably *should* think more about where I am and consider whether it is an appropriate moment to be cheering, but I can't help myself. I have a gut reaction. Is there something in your life that you always have a strong reaction to when you see it? Next time you feel that gut reaction to something adorable (a puppy or a baby) or something horrible (death or sickness) or something exciting (a home run by the Padres), remember this verse. Jesus had a *gut reaction* of

> **Jesus feels for His people. He doesn't feel for them in an abstract, forgetful way. He feels it in the very core of who He is.**

compassion for His children who are distressed and dejected.

Jesus feels for His people. He doesn't feel for them in an abstract, forgetful way. He feels what they feel. If His people feel discouraged, He understands that feeling and is touched by it: "For we do not have a high priest who is unable to sympathize with our weaknesses, but one who has been tempted in every way as we are, yet without sin" (Heb. 4:15). He sympathizes with us when we are down. He feels it in the very core of who He is.

We may not understand just how desperate the Israelites were at this point in history. Bible scholar Tokunboh Adeyemo helps us see the depth of their situation: "Politically, they bore the burden of heavy taxes, servitude, and human rights violations. Their religious leaders were not providing teaching, pastoral care or help with material needs. They endured leprosy, fevers, chronic illnesses, demon possession, blindness, paralysis, and many other troubles."[4] Our Good Shepherd looks at His sheep, and He yearns for them. He yearns to alleviate their suffering. He doesn't just want to alleviate their physical suffering, but their spiritual suffering as well. He wants them to experience wholeness, *shalom*.

Jesus' humanity shows in the urgency He conveys to His disciples as He sees the needs around them: *"Pray for more workers! These people need what we have to give!"* Jesus knew the needs of the world were going to be more than could be reached by a handful of disciples. He urges them to pray for more disciples, more workers, so that the "sheep without a shepherd" will be helped to find the true Good Shepherd.

Jesus' compassion always leads to action. Jesus didn't just look out at the crowd and think, *Oh, it's a bummer that they are sad. I hope things get better for them.* He looked to those around them and gave

Let Jesus open your eyes to the fact that He has been with you on the road all along.

them marching orders. "Pray! GO!" His ministry up to this point had been filled with compassionate acts. He had already been giving the blind sight. He had already been healing the sick. He had already been giving hope and life to those around Him. His compassion led Him to the discouraged in order to give them more and to ease the pain they felt.

Discouraged one, He sees you. He feels for you. He is compelled to help you. He is compelled to show you more of who He is. He will do what is necessary to make you strong in heart and faith, and He will not tire of loving you in this way. He will not tire of showing Himself gentle with you over and over again. I have experienced this gentleness, and I have especially experienced this compassion over the last few years. God has used His workers (pastors, friends, family, counselors) to be His workers for me. There is no shame in admitting you thought things would be different. Jesus encouraged the disciples on the road to Emmaus to give voice to their dashed hopes. He encourages you to do the same. Then let Him reveal Himself to you. Let Jesus open your eyes to the fact that He has been with you on the road all along. His gut reaction toward your discouragement isn't anger or disappointment. His gut reaction toward your discouragement is compassion. He wants to gather you to Himself and care for you. He is our Great Shepherd.

four

JESUS WITH
THE DENIERS

Peter showed his soul on the night when he denied knowing Jesus.
Or, as I prefer to think of it, when he finally told the truth.
CHAD BIRD

"Woman, I don't know him."
LUKE 22:57

You are probably familiar with the story of Peter denying Christ. But for those of you who need a refresher, let me set the scene. Peter had been following Christ as one of His disciples for years. He was one of the first Christ called to Himself: "As he was walking along the Sea of Galilee, he saw two brothers, Simon (who is called Peter), and his brother Andrew. They were casting a net into the sea—for they were fishermen. 'Follow me,' he told them, 'and I will make you fish for people.' Immediately they left their nets and followed him" (Matt. 4:18–20). From that early moment by the seashore when Christ first called Peter, Peter had followed Jesus faithfully—until the moment we will look at now. Peter loved Jesus. He prided himself on the fact that he was committed to Christ. So what went wrong? How did Peter get to the point where he denied knowing his teacher, whom he loved? Let's take a look at what led up to this moment.

THE LAST SUPPER

Jesus had served His disciples Communion. He warned them about His body being broken and His blood being shed. He had washed His disciples' feet, humbling Himself and attempting to prepare their hearts. Jesus had talked with them about what actually makes a human great—that serving and loving, giving and sacrificing, are what lay in store for those who choose His way. Jesus showed them the stark difference between what the world counts as strong and what would be required of them as followers of Christ.

The gospel of Luke narrates how Jesus turns His loving preparation to focus on Peter. Even before Peter commits the act of denial, Jesus demonstrates His tenderness by endeavoring to help Peter understand what was coming: "Simon, Simon, Satan has asked to sift you like wheat. But I have prayed for you that your faith may not fail. And you, when you have turned back, strengthen your brothers" (Luke 22:31–32). How astonishing! Before Jesus predicts that Peter will deny Him and before the denial takes place, Jesus tells Peter He is praying

> **Jesus lets Peter know that Satan and judgment won't have the last word. Grace will have the last word.**

for him. Jesus prays that in Peter's sin, in his denial, his faith won't fail. I find it interesting that Jesus doesn't say He prayed that Peter wouldn't deny Him. Jesus understands Peter's weakness. He understands what is coming next. Jesus lets Peter know that Satan and judgment won't have the last word. Grace will have the last word.

Jesus not only foresees Peter's denial, but He also foresees Peter's restoration. He calmly refers to "when you have turned back." Peter can't even imagine that he will have to turn back from anything or that his faith will fail for any reason, so he ostentatiously proclaims, "Lord, I am ready to go with you both to prison and to death" (v. 33). Jesus predicts Peter's failure, and Peter counters Jesus' prediction with a promise of unwavering devotion. Jesus responds, "I tell you, Peter, before the rooster crows today, you will deny three times that you know me" (v. 34 NIV). Jesus' statement is so devastatingly matter-of-fact. "No, Peter. You will not fight to the death. You will cower; you will deny. And the sound of a simple animal will be what brings you to your senses and to your knees."

THE FIRE

The predicted denials come, to be sure:

> Peter followed at a distance. And when some there had kindled a fire in the middle of the courtyard and had sat down together, Peter sat down with them. A servant girl saw him seated there in the firelight. She looked closely at him and said, "This man was with him."
>
> But he denied it. "Woman, I don't know him," he said.
>
> A little later someone else saw him and said, "You also are one of them."
>
> "Man, I am not!" Peter replied.

About an hour later another asserted, "Certainly this fellow was with him, for he is a Galilean."

Peter replied, "Man, I don't know what you're talking about!" Just as he was speaking, the rooster crowed. The Lord turned and looked straight at Peter. Then Peter remembered the word the Lord had spoken to him: "Before the rooster crows today, you will disown me three times." And he went outside and wept bitterly. (Luke 22:54–62 NIV)

We'd like to think that Peter had a moment of weakness, that somehow he forgot himself for just a second, that he was scared, that he wasn't thinking straight. But perhaps the truth of the matter is that Peter was finally expressing what he had deeply feared or felt all along. Maybe he finally came clean with himself and those around him. His confession, "I don't know him," *was* true. Peter didn't really know Jesus. He didn't yet really know forgiveness; he didn't really know grace. Peter was addicted to achieving. He loved to be the one right next to Jesus. He was outspoken in his devotion to Him. Peter was confident of his commitment to Christ. He didn't really understand that Christ's commitment to Peter was ultimately all that mattered. God's covenant toward Peter is what kept Peter close, not his own willpower. Peter really didn't know Jesus, but he was about to be introduced very soon. With the heat of shame burning in his face, Peter stood by the fire and called down curses just to prove to all those who could hear him that he was *not* a follower of Christ.

We have access to our faithful Savior. Our access—our acceptance by Him—isn't based on our faithfulness; it's based on His.

Then the rooster called him out.

And Peter went outside and wept bitterly.

Peter came to the end of himself. He came to the end of his own good opinion of himself. He came to the end of achieving. Later in life, Peter would have to repeatedly return to this death of self, but this first time was bitter indeed. I am sure you have felt the bitterness of being disappointed with yourself. I know I have. *Why would I do that? Why would I say that? Why would I react like that?* are words to the tune of an old song we are all familiar with. *I really thought I was better than that.* Peter thought he was better, and we think we are better than that as well. But the truth is we are denying sinners in need of a faithful Savior. The astonishingly lovely fact is that we have access to that Faithful Savior. Our access—our acceptance by Him—isn't based on our faithfulness; it's based on His.

THE LOOK

At this worst moment in Peter's life, Jesus was right there: "Just as he was speaking, the rooster crowed. The Lord turned and looked straight at Peter" (Luke 22:60–61 NIV).

What an absolute gut punch! In the middle of Peter's denial, Jesus turns and looks at Peter. One Bible's study notes explain:

> With the third denial, the rooster crows, just as Jesus predicted. In an additional touch of drama, the Lord looks at Peter, an act that indicates he knows what Peter has just done. Whether Jesus is being moved from one place to another at that time, can glance through a window, or is outside for a moment is not clear. The Lord's glance leads Peter to recall the prediction of a threefold denial. It is too much. He departs, weeping bitterly. His heart knows what he has done. The pain of his action expresses his real allegiance, a connection his lips cannot utter. Peter has experienced a

major failure of nerve. The Lord's word, as always, has come true. He knew Peter better than Peter did.[1]

Though Jesus knew Peter's every fault, Jesus chooses to look at him. Jesus doesn't choose to ignore or to break the relationship. He reminds Peter that He sees, and I can't imagine this look being anything but a look of love. Jesus isn't surprised by Peter's denial or sin. Jesus knew this was coming and had already told Peter He was praying for him. Christ's look of love draws Peter. The same love that drew Peter from the Sea of Galilee and a life of fishing draws him yet again. But this time Peter knows that he has failed and that he will not follow Jesus "to prison or to death." Peter runs. He weeps. He is undone.

But this isn't the end of the story.

THE RESTORATION

Remember how Jesus referred Peter to a time "when you have turned back"? Jesus doesn't leave Peter alone with his crushing disappointment with himself.

> [Jesus] revealed himself in this way . . . When daybreak came, Jesus stood on the shore, but the disciples did not know it was Jesus. "Friends," Jesus called to them, "you don't have any fish, do you?"
>
> "No," they answered.
>
> "Cast the net on the right side of the boat," he told them, "and you'll find some." So they did, and they were unable to haul it in because of the large number of fish. The disciple, the one Jesus loved, said to Peter, "It is the Lord!"
>
> When Simon Peter heard that it was the Lord, he tied his outer clothing around him (for he had taken it off) and

plunged into the sea. Since they were not far from land (about a hundred yards away), the other disciples came in the boat, dragging the net full of fish. . . .

"Come and have breakfast," Jesus told them. . . .

When they had eaten breakfast, Jesus asked Simon Peter, "Simon, son of John, do you love me more than these?"

"Yes, Lord," he said to him, "you know that I love you."

"Feed my lambs," he told him. A second time he asked him, "Simon, son of John, do you love me?"

"Yes, Lord," he said to him, "you know that I love you."

"Shepherd my sheep," he told him.

He asked him the third time, "Simon, son of John, do you love me?"

Peter was grieved that he asked him the third time, "Do you love me?" He said, "Lord, you know everything; you know that I love you."

"Feed my sheep," Jesus said. (John 21:1, 4–8, 12, 15–17)

There is a lot of speculation about why Jesus asked Peter three times if he loved Him and a lot of commentary about the different Greek words used in this back-and-forth conversation. The Lord has so plainly orchestrated Peter's faith journey! The Gospels display many interesting patterns in the relationship between Peter and Jesus. Jesus initially called Peter by the sea after a fishing session, and Jesus calls him back here again by the sea after a fishing session. The only two times a charcoal fire is mentioned is the one when Peter is denying Jesus, and the breakfast fire, where Jesus is restoring Peter. Peter denies Jesus three times; Peter says He loves Christ three times.

All these earlier interactions seem to lead to this important moment, though, when Jesus asks Peter for the third time, "Do

> Jesus *does* know. He knows the fickleness of our hearts. He knows we are fully committed to Him one day and wonder if He even cares the next.

you love me?" Peter is grieved, and he says this: "Lord, you know everything; you know that I love you." And there it is: Peter's confession. In effect, Peter is saying, "You know everything! You know how weak I am. You know I denied You. You know I did the very thing I promised I wouldn't do when I said, 'If all fall away from You, I won't. I will go to prison or even die for You.' But Lord, You also know I do love You. My love is feeble, but You know it is there." This is what I want you all to see. Jesus *does* know. He knows the fickleness of our hearts. He knows we are fully committed to Him one day and then wonder if He even cares the next day, or maybe that happens minute to minute.

But look how Jesus responded to Peter! Jesus doesn't tell Peter, "Listen, Peter, you made a huge mistake. I am going to need you to work on your devotion to Me before I am willing to use you." No, Jesus just tells Peter to get to the work of loving his neighbor and taking care of those around him: "The fact that Peter was clearly forgiven by Jesus and given new responsibilities, amounting to apostleship, despite his total denial of his Lord, can give genuine hope to Christians today who feel that they have denied Jesus and that this is unforgiveable. He calls only for our repentance and our love."[2]

Beloved, the level of your devotion isn't what makes God faithful to you or makes Him keep loving you. He is and always will be a faithful God to His people. This issue is never first our love for Christ, but rather His love for us. His love causes love.

Denier, He cares for you and loves you and will use you to love others.

five

JESUS WITH THE FAINTHEARTED

But no one except Lucy knew that as it circled the mast it had whispered to her, "Courage, dear heart," and the voice, she felt sure, was Aslan's, and with the voice a delicious smell breathed in her face.

C. S. LEWIS

He cried, "Master, save me!" Jesus didn't hesitate. He reached down and grabbed his hand. Then he said, "Faint-heart, what got into you?"

MATTHEW 14:30–31 MSG

Have you ever watched a child learn how to ride a bike? It is a precarious situation at best. Most children, unless they are born daredevils, are intensely fearful. This fear is understandable and legitimate. The ground is unforgiving, the fall feels long, and balance is something that must be learned. The problem is that the more a child gives in to the fear of falling, the more likely they are to fall, but that is a difficult lesson to learn and one that doesn't make sense to a four-year-old (or a forty-year-old, now that I think about it). But what most children also can't see or comprehend is that their caregiver or teacher is just as invested in them staying upright as they are. The teacher is generally running behind the child with hands outstretched, trying their hardest to make sure that the bike and the child on that bike doesn't tip. All the while, that teacher is yelling, "You can do it! Pedal! Pedal! I've got you." The teacher knows the child needs confidence, but that same invested coach also knows the child needs support and help in case they fall. The child needs confidence in themselves but also confidence in the helper to be right there if anything goes awry. The moment confidence diminishes, the wobbles set in; the bike and rider are bound to crash. Riding a bike isn't just a physical feat, it is an emotional one as well.

While I am sure that riding a bike and walking on water are not the same experience, both take a significant kind of heart courage to accomplish.

I NEED A NEW MIRACLE

It was Peter, of course, who decided to try out his skill as a water walker. Though all the Gospels tell the story of Jesus' ministry, the story about Peter's trip out on the sea is only recorded in Matthew. Mark and John tell the same story about Jesus walking on the water, but they leave out the part about Peter's attempt.

In the timeline of Jesus' ministry, this event takes place right after Jesus feeds five thousand men, plus women and children, with only five loaves of bread and two fish:

Immediately [Jesus] made the disciples get into the boat
and go ahead of him to the other side, while he dismissed
the crowds. After dismissing the crowds, he went up on the
mountain by himself to pray. Well into the night, he was
there alone. Meanwhile, the boat was already some distance
from land, battered by the waves, because the wind was
against them. (Matt. 14:22–24)

Get the scene set in your imagination. Jesus has just performed
this wondrous miracle. Everyone is on an emotional high following this physics-defying work of Jesus: "When the people saw
the sign he had done, they said, 'This truly is the Prophet who is
to come into the world.' Therefore, when Jesus realized that they
were about to come and take him by force to make him king, he
withdrew again to the mountain by himself" (John 6:14–15).
Jesus could feel that the Jewish people were wanting Him to take
political power; they misunderstood His mission. They were going to force Him to be the king they wanted, so wisely Jesus withdrew. I love this picture of Christ. The people thought the point of
His power was to gain an earthly rule, but
Jesus disdains earthly power. The point of **Christ's mission wasn't a**
the miracle was to care for the needy, the **power grab. His mission**
poor, and the hungry. His mission wasn't a **was to live sacrificially**
power grab. His mission was to live sacrifi- **and die so others might**
cially and die so others might live wholly. **live wholly.**
Essentially, Jesus excuses Himself from
the situation. He goes to the place where
He is known and loved—intimacy with the Father. He withdraws
to pray. He tells His disciples to go ahead without Him. The word-
ing here is very strong: "He made the disciples get into the boat
and go ahead of him."

Not only had the disciples just seen this intense miracle, but they had also witnessed the crowd wanting Jesus to assert His power for political gain. Think how frazzled and bewildered they must have felt as Jesus rushed them away. Then they get into the boat, and an intense storm appears to top off this wild afternoon.

Here is where we pick up the story: "Jesus came toward them walking on the sea very early in the morning. When the disciples saw him walking on the sea, they were terrified. 'It's a ghost!' they said, and they cried out in fear" (Matt. 14:25–26).

Now I don't know about you, but their reaction seems legitimate to me! Their day has been an emotional one, to say the least. They are out on the water, fighting against the waves, and they see someone walking toward them—on the water! No wonder they are terrified. No wonder they think Jesus is a ghost.

HAVE COURAGE

"Immediately Jesus spoke to them. 'Have courage! It is I. Don't be afraid'" (Matt. 14:27). Jesus reveals Himself to them and gives them two instructions: have courage and don't be afraid. The language Jesus uses to refer to Himself intentionally underlines His oneness with His Father, the great "I AM":

> The expression "It is I" (lit., "I am") may allude to the voice of Yahweh from the burning bush (Ex. 3:14) and the voice of assurance to Israel of the Lord's identity and presence as their Savior (Isa. 43:10–13). Throughout this section Jesus continues to reveal his true nature to the disciples, and this powerful statement accords with his miraculous calming of the storm."[1]

"Have courage. It is I. Don't be afraid." With those three sentences Jesus speaks a word into your storms as well. His message to the disciples is His message to you. Have faith and trust in who He is. Peter hears this message and responds radically, which is right in line with his personality.

> Jesus' message to the disciples is His message to you. Have faith and trust in who He is.

"IF IT IS YOU"

Peter isn't sure what's happening: "'Lord, if it's you,' Peter answered him, 'command me to come to you on the water.' He said, 'Come.' And climbing out of the boat, Peter started walking on the water and came toward Jesus" (Matt. 14:28–29).

I love how Peter isn't completely sure. His faith isn't sure and complete. That's a big "if"—*if* it is you. Peter thinks he's seeing Jesus, but he isn't sure. His heart is showing signs of faintness. But Jesus calls him—just as He did when He first told Peter to follow Him, just as He did when He restored Peter to fellowship and leadership in ministry. He says it again: "Come, Peter. Follow."

Peter responds by doing a totally Peter thing. He climbs out of the boat and starts walking on water. He is doing the impossible! It's too easy to forget that the disciples were real humans with real emotions and real thoughts. Put yourself in Peter's place for just a second. Think through the day you have had. Three seconds ago, you were sure you saw a ghost. Now you think it is your rabbi. And now you are walking on water—the very same water that was battering your boat just a few minutes ago, the same water that was a source of great fear. Now you are standing on it. How? You stop looking at Jesus and look around. Realization hits you. You see and remember where you are.

"BUT WHEN HE SAW"

It must only have taken seconds for excitement and impulse to fade, replaced by sheer terror. Matthew's narrative describes it: "But when he saw the strength of the wind, he was afraid, and beginning to sink" (Matt. 14:30). Peter, who initially acted in the excitement of seeing Jesus, suddenly becomes overwhelmed by what his eyes see and what his body feels. He begins to sink.

> We are not told how far or for how long he walks on the sea, but suddenly reality hits. He sees the wind, meaning the effects of the wind, produce billowing whitecaps, surging seas, and wind-blown spray, and he realizes where he is and becomes afraid. Experienced fisherman that he is, he knows the danger. Peter demonstrates tremendous courage in this incident, but at the same time his courage to go to Jesus on the water becomes the occasion for failure. He loses his focused faith in Jesus' divine identity and begins to sink beneath the seas.[2]

We are so much like Peter. We naturally lose sight of what our focal point should be. We look around us. We see the brokenness of our lives and think, *There is no way I can follow Jesus where He wants me to go.* In a sense we remember who we are, and we know our own incapacity and weakness—and we doubt His strength. We set our sights on all the things that tell us that we can't do something, and we forget the One who did it all for us. We are fainthearted. We want to obey but we are scared. We lose faith. We forget why we decided getting out of the boat was a good idea to begin with. We get the feeling the bike we are on is going to tip—and the fall is really going to hurt.

PETER CRIED OUT

Even though Peter's faith isn't at its strongest here, it is still intact. He knows where to call for help. Matthew 14:30 says, "He cried out, 'Lord, save me!'"

Peter utters the words we all cry out when the storm is overwhelming and we feel we are sinking: "Lord, save me!" Even in the middle of his doubting, Peter knew Jesus was the One who could save him.

> **In our weak, uncertain, failing moments, we get the point: Jesus is there to save us.**

This story encourages my heart! The point isn't Peter's faith. It never was! The point is that we have a Savior who delights in saving us. Jesus calls us, and even when we follow, we will stumble and fail. In those weak, uncertain, failing moments, we get that real point: Jesus is there to save us. We don't have to get down on ourselves for not having the faith to keep walking. Peter didn't have enough confident faith. We don't, either. So often believers are encouraged to be "faith-filled," to cultivate a strong and courageous faith. But we all know it's not so easy. Peter's strong and courageous faith came and went. When Peter was sinking, his faith was small. But the Savior's strength didn't depend on how big Peter's faith was. Jesus' willingness and strength to save is forever written into His character; the Savior is who He is.

I am sure you can think of a time in your life when you cried out for saving, not positive if or when that rescue would come. You were hoping against all hope that no matter what the circumstances were that somehow you would be saved from the storm-tossed sea and that you would be able to walk when you should have been drowning. Peter didn't have to admit his failure before Jesus would save him. Peter just admitted his need. This is always what Christ requires. Agree with Him about the assessment of your life: you and I need help, and we need it from Him!

FAINT-HEART

How often have you felt yourself to be "fainthearted"? In this story, Peter is the fainthearted disciple: "Jesus didn't hesitate. He reached down and grabbed his hand. Then he said, 'Faint-heart, what got into you?'" (Matt. 14:31 MSG).

Immediately, Jesus did what He takes delight in doing: He reached down and grabbed Peter. The saving comes first before Jesus goes on to ask, "Why did you doubt? Where is your faith? What got into you?" Peter believed. We believe. But Peter doubted, and we doubt. Jesus forgives our unbelief that exists alongside our belief. He calls to the faith in us. He resurrects our faith as He reaches down and rescues us from the depths.

> Jesus immediately catches Peter by the hand to rescue him and says, "You of little faith, why did you doubt?" "Little faith" (*oligopistos*) is not the same as the "no faith" of the hard-hearted townspeople of Nazareth (13:58). A person with no faith would not recognize Jesus and call out to him. Peter has faith; it is just not functioning properly. It is "ineffective faith" (cf. 17:20). Peter's faith enables him to recognize Jesus' true identity and to request to come out to him on the water, but it is like a burst of emotional energy. It is effective enough to motivate him but not effective enough to sustain him. The key element is keeping his eyes firmly focused on Jesus instead of the danger of the wind-swept sea. Jesus thus directs Peter to understand more clearly who he is and then act upon it. Faith is not like a commodity of which Peter needs more. Rather, faith is consistent trust in Jesus to accomplish what Peter is called to do.[3]

Jesus doesn't refuse to help Peter until Peter's faith is effective. Jesus saves Peter right in the middle of Peter's doubt. Jesus reaches down and takes His fainthearted disciple and brings him to safety. This is good news for us. This is the grace that exudes from the heart of Jesus. He doesn't say, "Look Peter. I literally just fed thousands of people with five fish and two loaves of bread. I am standing here on the water—water I shouldn't be able to stand on. I am standing on it. I walked across this whole body of water to get to you. Through a storm. Why would you ever doubt My power? Come on! Get your act together! Repent before I save you!"

No, this is not who Jesus is. He just saves Peter and reminds him that Jesus is worth every single ounce of trust and faith that can be mustered. "Why did you doubt?" isn't a question that Jesus needs answered for Himself. Jesus knows why Peter doubted. He knows why you and I doubt. We are weak. Jesus asked the question so Peter could remind himself that he doesn't need to doubt. Jesus lifts Peter's eyes again. He asks Peter to focus on Him.

> In our doubt, He saves us. In our fear, He rescues us. In our faintheartedness, He empathizes with us and calls us into safety.

Jesus is not only powerful, but He is full of grace as well. He had performed miracles immediately before the boat incident that *should* have made Peter's faith solid, but Jesus knows us well. He knows our weak and fickle hearts—and He continues to call us to Himself. In our doubt, He saves us. In our fear, He rescues us. In our faintheartedness, He empathizes with us and calls us into safety.

Fainthearted one, have courage. Do not be afraid. Jesus is with you in the storm. He is with you in your doubts. Your doubts and lack of faith do not disqualify you from His love and grace. Take your eyes off the storm. Look at your Savior, who beckons you to come. You will find safety there. He is strong enough to handle it all.

six

JESUS WITH THE FAILURE

We don't love little because we have little that requires forgiveness.
We love little because we have confessed little and hidden much.
DANIEL PRICE

When the Pharisee who had invited him saw this, he said to himself,
"This man, if he were a prophet, would know who and what kind
of woman this is who is touching him—she's a sinner!"
MATTHEW 7:39

W e don't advertise it on social media, for sure, but most of
us have known failure—or even used the word, if only in
our own minds, to describe ourselves. The failure, deep in self-
accusation as well as the less-than-admiring perception of those

around them, tends to stay away from others. It hurts too much to be out and about with a damaged self-regard or a damaged public reputation.

But the gospel of Luke gives us an account of a time when a failure came to Jesus:

> Then one of the Pharisees invited him to eat with him. He entered the Pharisee's house and reclined at the table. And a woman in the town who was a sinner found out that Jesus was reclining at the table in the Pharisee's house. She brought an alabaster jar of perfume and stood behind him at his feet, weeping, and began to wash his feet with her tears. She wiped his feet with her hair, kissing them and anointing them with the perfume.
>
> When the Pharisee who had invited him saw this, he said to himself, "This man, if he were a prophet, would know who and what kind of woman this is who is touching him—she's a sinner!"
>
> Jesus replied to him, "Simon, I have something to say to you."
>
> He said, "Say it, teacher."
>
> "A creditor had two debtors. One owed five hundred denarii, and the other fifty. Since they could not pay it back, he graciously forgave them both. So, which of them will love him more?"
>
> Simon answered, "I suppose the one he forgave more."
>
> "You have judged correctly," he told him. Turning to the woman, he said to Simon, "Do you see this woman? I entered your house; you gave me no water for my feet, but she, with her tears, has washed my feet and wiped them with her hair. You gave me no kiss, but she hasn't

stopped kissing my feet since I came in. You didn't anoint my head with olive oil, but she has anointed my feet with perfume. Therefore I tell you, her many sins have been forgiven; that's why she loved much. But the one who is forgiven little, loves little." Then he said to her, "Your sins are forgiven."

Those who were at the table with him began to say among themselves, "Who is this man who even forgives sins?"

And he said to the woman, "Your faith has saved you. Go in peace." (Luke 7:36–50)

THE PEOPLE

Our story from Luke 7 has three main characters. First, Simon, a true Pharisee. Pharisees were considered the religious elite of that time. Think of him as a real Instagram influencer type who had it all together. Think of the Christian persona you might see on the social media platforms and immediately think, *He or she is really killing it.* It's that person who seems to always look perfect, with surroundings that always seem to look perfect, who never makes a mistake. That is our Simon.

The second character in our story is Jesus, our hero.

The third character is the failure—an uninvited guest known throughout the town as a sinner. When she hears Jesus is going to Simon's house, she grabs an alabaster jar of perfume and heads straight there, compelled to see Jesus.

Simon was known for being clean and doing right.
The woman was known for being dirty and doing wrong.

Simon was known for being religious.
The woman was known as a sinner.

Simon was known for keeping all the rules.
The woman was known as the one who broke all the rules.

Simon was known as a successful go-getter.
The woman was known as a failure.

When the failure "found out that Jesus was reclining at the table in the Pharisee's house," she didn't stay at home with her soiled reputation as damaged goods (v. 36). "She brought an alabaster jar of perfume and stood behind him at his feet, weeping, and began to wash his feet with her tears. She wiped his feet with her hair, kissing them and anointing them with the perfume" (vv. 37–38).

Can you imagine this social situation? Every eye in the room would be on the combination of the rabbi guest and the uninvited intruder—especially the eyes of the host, Simon: "When the Pharisee who had invited him saw this, he said to himself, 'This man, if he were a prophet, would know who and what kind of woman this is who is touching him—she's a sinner!'" (v. 39).

HOW SIMON TREATED JESUS

Simon was skeptical. In general, the Pharisees were not big fans of Jesus, the recently popular wandering prophet-teacher. In fact, the verses immediately preceding this story in the very same chapter of Luke contain some very direct words Jesus had to say about the Pharisees and the way they were responding to Him. Jesus criticized these religious leaders, who were determined to have something negative to say about anyone trying to teach the people besides themselves. Very likely, the host, Simon, being part of this group, regarded Jesus in a condescending way—a guest, certainly, but one inferior in standing to himself. During this visit, Jesus mentions Simon's failure to offer to wash his guest's dusty feet or to offer Him a kiss of welcome and other gracious outward acts of respect. From all the indicators of this story, it's safe to infer that Simon basically thinks he is better than Jesus.

HOW DID THE WOMAN TREAT JESUS?

Jesus and the religious leaders were reclining and eating at the table when she entered the room. A Bible commentary describes this common dining arrangement: "The Jews reclined on broad couches. Each man rested on his left elbow, his feet extended away from the table, kind of like a u shape and several persons occupied one couch."[1] Jesus' feet would have been behind Him, away from the central table of food.

Put yourself in the place of this uninvited woman. What was she thinking as she moved forward toward Jesus? She'd have known of Jesus' reputation for interacting with all kinds of people, and His growing reputation as a wise teacher and miraculous healer. Could she really be forgiven and accepted? Was this grace really for *her*? Could it really be that where sin abounded, grace would abound all the more (Rom. 5:20)?

The woman couldn't control her desire to be close to Jesus any longer. She went to His feet and started weeping. She washed His feet with her tears and dried them with her hair. This wasn't a couple of teardrops she immediately wiped away. This was an ugly cry—enough tears to wash feet with. Her actions went way, way beyond social awkwardness. Her behavior was scandalous. We kind of get the idea since this behavior would be pretty scandalous today. But this woman's actions would have been far more scandalous during the time of Jesus' ministry. For this woman even to let her hair down was a huge taboo; this was an act reserved for married women, only to be done when alone with their husbands.

For a woman just to enter this house and approach Jesus would have shocked everyone. Men were allowed to come and watch the religious people eat and even to listen to their conversation from the periphery of the room. But stepping forward was not done—and never, ever done if you were a woman.

> It doesn't matter that this woman didn't have words to express her grief, her relief, her gratitude, or her worship. Jesus' response elevates the rawness of emotions.

So what could have been so important to her—more important than following social norms, more important than remaining in the shadows with her sins? What drew the failure close to Jesus?

Presumably the woman had heard the message of forgiveness Jesus had been preaching across Palestine. Maybe she had heard that Jesus treated women differently, even with love and acceptance. She just knew Jesus had what she needed. So, our friend the failure comes to the feet of Jesus, weeping.

The Psalms describe that our tears are kept and our troubles counted by God (Ps. 56:8). The tears this woman weeps are precious to her Savior. In gratitude and worship, the woman kisses His feet. Overwhelmed by the gift of acceptance He has given her, she pours perfume on His feet. The woman gives what she has to Jesus.

It doesn't matter that this woman didn't have the words to express her grief, her relief, her gratitude, or her worship. Jesus' response to her elevates the rawness of emotions here. Not once does Jesus shame her for being an "emotional woman." He cherishes her gift of love, tears, kisses, and perfume. While the very idea makes us feel a little uncomfortable, Jesus doesn't exhibit any discomfort. Jesus remained completely at peace during this exchange. He wasn't uncomfortable at all.

Spurgeon wrote about this interchange between Jesus and this failed woman:

> Not a word, I say, came from her; and, brethren, we would prefer a single speechless lover of Jesus, who acted as she did, to ten thousand noisy talkers who have no gifts, no heart, no tears. As for the Master, he remained quietly acquiescent, saying nothing, but all the while drinking in her love, and letting his poor weary heart find sweet solace in the gratitude of one who once was a sinner, but who was to be such no more.[2]

Spurgeon seems to echo these words from 1 Corinthians 13, the "love" chapter:

> If I speak in the tongues of men or of angels, but do not have love, I am only a resounding gong or a clanging cymbal. If I have the gift of prophecy and can fathom all mysteries and all knowledge, and if I have a faith that can move mountains, but do not have love, I am nothing. If I give all I possess to the poor and give over my body to hardship that I may boast, but do not have love, I gain nothing.
> (1 Cor. 13:1–3 NIV)

All too often we prize measured intellect, having the right words to say, possessing extraordinary faith, or even giving of our finances. But our God prizes love. He says you can know all the right words and even do all the right things, but if you aren't doing it from a heart of love, then it is for nothing.

Jesus elevates and accepts this show of emotional gratitude. Where we would look away or think, "Wow! That is totally improper," Jesus receives and values her love. He doesn't look at her as an overly emotional woman who needs to get her act together.

HOW DOES JESUS TREAT SIMON?

While this display of love is going on, Jesus also loves Simon, the host, enough to address his wrong thoughts. Simon is watching what is happening and thinking, *If this man were a prophet like so many are saying he is, if he knew anything at all, he would know who is touching him! He would know she is a sinner.* So, Jesus replies to his thoughts, "Simon, I have something to say to you" (Luke 7:39–40). Jesus knows what Simon is thinking. Simon is ecstatic—smug because he thinks he has finally caught Jesus red-handed. "If he were a prophet, he would know who this woman was." Simon believes he is going to be the one who exposes Jesus for the fraud the Pharisees believed Him to be.

Surprise, Simon! Jesus does know who the woman is. Next level surprise: Jesus knows who you are, too, Simon. Simon is the one who doesn't know who he is talking to.

THE PARABLE

The woman knows Jesus. Jesus knows the woman. Jesus knows Simon. Simon is clueless. Jesus uses a parable to take Simon on a brief trip of self-reflection—and to show him who he is actually talking to.

Jesus tells a story about two people who owe money. One person owes a considerable amount more than the other, but the bottom line is neither one can pay. The lender looks at them both and releases them of their obligation to pay. Then he asks Simon this question so Simon can know himself: "Who is more grateful? Who loves more?"

Simon hates to answer this, but he gives it up: "I suppose the one who owed more."

No doubt Simon is thinking that, with his squeaky-clean reputation and his social status, he's definitely the debtor who owes less and is forgiven less. But Jesus gently points to evidence that Simon is actually the one who owes more. Simon didn't wash Jesus' feet. Simon didn't greet Jesus with a traditional kiss. He didn't anoint his guest with perfume. But that "damaged goods" woman came into Simon's house and treated Jesus the way He deserved to be treated—washing His feet with her own tears, lavishing His feet with kisses, and the sacrificial gift of the perfume.

Jesus explains why the "failure" woman is so overwhelmed with love and gratitude. She has been forgiven much so she loves much. This woman was honest about her sin and received the greatest gift.

HOW DOES JESUS TREAT THE WOMAN?

Jesus isn't ashamed of this woman or embarrassed by what she is doing. He calls attention to her. "Simon . . . Do you see this woman?" Jesus doesn't just accept and forgive her. He sticks up for her! Jesus becomes her advocate, so she doesn't have to stand up for herself. Jesus stands between the accuser and the woman. He says to Simon, in effect, "Your accusations must come through me. I see her. I see what she is doing. I approve."

> Jesus doesn't just accept and forgive her. He sticks up for her! Jesus becomes her advocate.

Whatever failures trouble your memories, whatever flaws you wish your friends and neighbors would never see, Jesus defends you too. Jesus is our advocate. John writes about it: "My little children, I am writing you these things so that you may not sin. But if anyone does sin, we have an advocate with the Father—Jesus Christ the righteous one. He himself is the atoning sacrifice for our sins, and not only for ours, but also for those of the whole world" (1 John 2:1–2).

Who stands before you and condemns you? Do you condemn yourself? Do others condemn you? Does the enemy repeatedly remind you of all your past faults and sins? Jesus is your advocate. He pleads your case. His life, death, resurrection, the gift of His righteousness given to you—it all means you stand before God now as wholly loved, accepted, and forgiven. Who can condemn you when God Himself justifies you?

Jesus justified this woman—the one everyone else considered a disreputable sinner.

TOO GOOD OR TOO BAD

We are not very good at seeing ourselves clearly, but do you think you are one who loves little or loves much? The way you answer this question will depend on how you see yourself and how you see God.

How do you see yourself? Do these thought patterns have a familiar ring?

> *I mean, I have some bad days, but I am not like those people!*
>
> *They voted for . . . ! ?*
>
> *Did you hear what she said? Did you see where he went?*
>
> *Everyone knows that person is a sinner. Just look at that Facebook profile!*
>
> *To be honest, God is pretty lucky to have me.*
>
> *Did you see what I did?*
>
> *Did you see how I was honored?*
>
> *Did you see how everyone thinks of me?*

Most of us tend to judge ourselves gently, thinking, *I'm pretty good—and certainly not a failure. I don't really need to approach God.* There are times we just don't think we need to weep at Jesus' feet.

At other times we feel too much shame—and that also keeps us from approaching the Savior:

> *I know God sees where I went.*
>
> *I know God knows what I thought.*
>
> *I know God knows the website I visited.*
>
> *I know God sees my addiction.*
>
> *I know God witnesses every failure.*
>
> *I have done too much that is wrong.*
>
> *I have gone too far.*
>
> *I am such a colossal failure.*
>
> *I can't approach God.*

What a blessing that the gospel writer Luke shows us Jesus interacting with this "woman who loved much." This "failure" rejected both unhelpful lines of thinking. She is all too aware she isn't too good to come to Jesus, but she is also aware that her badness doesn't need to keep her away. She hoped in the Savior and came to Jesus, falling at His feet in repentance and devotion—loving much. Her act of penitence and gratitude demonstrates her awareness of her own sin and her right focus on the Savior.

THE PROCLAMATION: YOUR SINS ARE FORGIVEN

Simon thought he had few or no sins. He was pretty sure he was killing it. Of course, outwardly he seemed to be pulling it off, but his encounter with Jesus—when he failed to show Jesus respect and proper welcome in his home—showed evidence of the inward absence of love.

In his self-confidence and pride in his social and religious standing, Simon decided which rules he wanted to follow. When he didn't, he justified himself by telling himself those rules didn't really apply to a worthy person like him.

Don't we all do this?

> *I know I shouldn't speak poorly about her, but . . .*
>
> *I know I shouldn't respond out of anger, but . . .*
>
> *I know I shouldn't drive in the carpool lane when it is just me, but I can't be late.*
>
> *I know I shouldn't go to that website, but . . .*
>
> *I know I shouldn't . . .*

Simon looked down on the woman—and anyone else who didn't live the way he did. He loved little because he thought he didn't owe much. Simon didn't need to go out and commit some big sins in order to love Jesus more. He needed to acknowledge that his own heart was just as dark as the woman's. He needed to see that he actually *was* a person who owed much. Simon was as complete a failure as the "sinful" woman was. His sins of pride, judgment, and self-justification were equal to anything she was doing out in the city.

Thinking you are sinless—or, at least, better than everyone else—will make you a critical, angry person. You will find your joy in thinking of yourself in mostly positive terms instead of finding your joy in thinking of yourself as a forgiven and loved sinner who is now an accepted and approved saint.

Dan Price says this:

The big love of Jesus can give forever and never run dry. But because we live from a position of lack, we cannot fathom that anyone has enough love, grace, and goodness to fill up the account of even just one *real* sinner (never mind a whole world of them). So we actively try to show we're not overly deficient. We push to the front of the line, walk right up, and present ourselves as one who needs only the smallest amount of grace. Our list of sins is short, and none of them are the really bad ones. As if to say: "Just top us off, Jesus. We've done pretty well." We have little that requires forgiveness. This is how we got here. This is how Simon got here. And this is how we all become ruled by little-love."[3]

The supposed failure in this story was not ruled by "little love." She clearly saw who she was and—even better!—who Jesus was. Loving much, she came to Jesus' feet and found her advocate.

How do you become someone who loves much? By understanding how much you have been forgiven. Revel in the goodness you see in the way Jesus treated a "failure." Stop comparing yourself with others. Instead, focus on the perfect life of Christ. The standard of Christ's perfection instantly shows how desperately we fall short.

When is the last time you were wowed by the love of Christ? It was probably the last time you screwed up badly but then also realized Jesus had grace for you. As we come close to the Savior, we understand more and more that sin isn't just something we do outwardly but it's the bent of our hearts. It's human nature to justify and please ourselves. Selfishness, glory stealing, attention seeking, inward focus—these make up our

> Loving Jesus much begins with seeing His generosity and becoming fully dependent on His generosity.

primary operating system. While we're busy patting ourselves on the back for not committing any *big* sins, we're missing our own desperate need of forgiveness for the sin of thinking we don't need a Savior because we aren't really all that bad.

Loving Jesus much begins with seeing His generosity and becoming fully dependent on His generosity. Luke rounds out the story of Jesus' encounter with this woman with Christ's declaration of her forgiveness. He tells her, "Your faith has saved you." She knew she was loved. Her faith was a gift—a saving gift. Then he says, "Go in peace." They are reconciled. He has restored her to wholeness. She has peace with God. She has been invited near. The one who had been far off and excluded is now welcome at the table. Praise God this woman didn't get so caught up in her own sin that she forgot who her Savior was. In spite of herself—and her knowledge of herself—she was able to receive the love and acceptance of Jesus. With Jesus as advocate, she no longer needed to strive or to prove herself. She could be at peace.

"You are forgiven," Jesus pronounced, right in front of the religious community. She knew it already—that was why she was overwhelmed and weeping at His feet. But Jesus proclaimed it in front of the religious so they would know her new status: she was no longer to be known as a sinner but had been renamed as a woman who was forgiven. She could go in peace—peace with her Savior and restored peace with her neighbors and community.

We have a Redeemer who pays all the debts. You are free.

Do you want to love big? Do you want to love more? Has your self-appraisal of being too good or too bad kept you away from the feet of Jesus? In Jesus' teaching parable for Simon, both the debtors are forgiven—much and little. The point is, we have a

Redeemer who pays all the debts. Jesus says the same words to you that He said to Simon and the woman all those years ago: "Your debt has been paid." You are released from the tyranny to pay back what you once owed. You are free. Live in that freedom. Love others out of that freedom. Forgive others because you have been forgiven so very much.

There is freedom and forgiveness for the failure. Hear the words of Jesus to you, "Your sins are forgiven. Your faith has saved you. Go in peace."

seven

JESUS WITH THE FEARFUL

He knew what fear was all about—the scalp cold, the mouth dry,
the midnight knock at the door—but he also knew that fear was not
the last thing. It was the next to the last thing. The last thing was hope.
FREDERICK BUECHNER

"Indeed, the hairs of your head are all counted. Don't be afraid;
you are worth more than many sparrows."
LUKE 12:7

F ear, like most emotions, can be helpful or hurtful. It can be an
indicator that danger is near and motivate us to get out of a
perilous situation. Fear can be a good thing. It can also exaggerate
situations. Fear can make us think a threat is real when the threat

isn't as much as we make it out to be. Fear can be a liar. We need wisdom to help us understand our fears and to respond to them appropriately.

The people following Jesus—His chosen disciples and many others reaching out for the truth and wisdom and authority in His teaching—had fears like ours. Some of those fears were disproportionate to reality, while others were quite in line with the societal and political and interpersonal dangers around them. And Jesus—wisdom embodied—noted and addressed their fears. The teaching of our wise Savior can help us understand and respond to fears.

Jesus' teaching realigned people's perceptions about fear—and about what is worth fearing:

> "I say to you, my friends, don't fear those who kill the body, and after that can do nothing more. But I will show you the one to fear: Fear him who has authority to throw people into hell after death. Yes, I say to you, this is the one to fear! Aren't five sparrows sold for two pennies? Yet not one of them is forgotten in God's sight. Indeed, the hairs of your head are all counted. Don't be afraid; you are worth more than many sparrows." (Luke 12:4–7)

Jesus is talking to His disciples, who were experiencing some trouble as they stood up to the religious leaders of that day. Luke has just narrated a strong word of rebuke that Jesus had for those very religious leaders (Luke 11:37–53). By "strong word" I mean Jesus really nailed the Pharisees with "Woe to you!" and thoroughly communicated that He detested the way they loved power. Jesus rejected their system that would force people to live up to all their extra rules instead of leadership by loving people right where they

Christianity, the Jesus way, rejects the path of power.

were. Jesus was never one to mince words, and He went right after the people in power.

This approach really goes against our natural inclination, doesn't it? We naturally think the place to be is in the good graces of those already in charge. We love to be in with the people in power because it brings us a sense of safety and taste of the power. Christianity, the Jesus way, rejects the path of power. Jesus always identified with the weak and the vulnerable. Jesus had no time or desire to kiss up to the ones in charge of religious practice.

Jesus prized truth over power. Jesus also knew that His priorities would put Him and His disciples in danger. The gospel of Luke describes how the trouble started: "When he left there, the scribes and the Pharisees began to oppose him fiercely and to cross-examine him about many things; they were lying in wait for him to trap him in something he said" (Luke 11:53–54). The religious leaders of the day were already out to get Him; it hadn't taken long at all.

Jesus openly instructs His followers to avoid the hypocrisy of these religious leaders, pointing out how the Pharisees act as if they are spiritual and godly while really, they are just out to hurt others and hold on to their position and good name. Jesus speaks very plainly:

> "Be on your guard against the leaven of the Pharisees, which is hypocrisy. There is nothing covered that won't be uncovered, nothing hidden that won't be made known. Therefore, whatever you have said in the dark will be heard in the light, and what you have whispered in an ear in private rooms will be proclaimed on the housetops." (Luke 12:1–3)

Jesus is reminding His disciples—and us—that everything we think is a secret, every motivation, every thought, will one day be laid bare before God.

Jesus wants His followers to show fear and reverence toward God more than they fear anything that earthly leaders might do to them. As He charges His disciples not to be afraid, He's telling them, "Don't be afraid to speak out against injustice. Don't be afraid to speak out against power. Don't be afraid to call a thing what it is." But He has a different reason for why they shouldn't fear. That's why He doesn't say, "Don't be afraid because you won't get hurt," or "Don't be afraid because nothing bad will happen to you." Jesus knows that His teaching is already causing the trouble that will lead to danger for all of them. He knew the people He was calling out as hypocrites were going to silence Him in the most permanent way they knew how—by killing Him. Still, Jesus tells His disciples, "Don't be afraid."

MY FRIENDS

Jesus begins by calling His disciples "my friends." Can you sense the emotion behind this term of endearment, used as He is about to give them a difficult yet comforting instruction. This is the first instance in the book of Luke where Jesus refers to His disciples as His friends. "'All things are common to friends,' according to the ancient ideal, and the commonality in view here apparently includes shared enemies, shared fate at the hands of those who spurn God's purpose for themselves, and shared knowledge," writes one commentator on the book of Luke.[1] Jesus knew what lay ahead for Himself and His disciples. It wasn't an easy road ahead. Eleven of the twelve Jesus was addressing would one day be martyred or would suffer greatly until their deaths. The exception was Judas, who opted to throw

Jesus understands the price we must pay when we stand up for the upside-down kingdom of God.

in his lot with the powerful leaders Jesus was speaking out against. Judas's fate was even more horrific than that of the others. He died by hanging himself, alone in a field, with a heart full of regret (Matt. 27:1–10).

By calling them friends, Jesus communicated right away that He had real affection for His disciples. More than the affection a teacher has for his students, Jesus felt a shared commonality with them. He knew that their decision to follow Him was not an easy one and He loves them as friends. He loves you as a friend too. He understands the price we must pay when we stand up for the upside-down kingdom of God. He understands the danger that comes when speaking to power.

WHO TO FEAR?

Jesus doesn't diminish the danger His disciple friends face. He knows the leaders they are opposing can "kill the body." But Jesus makes them aware of a greater reality, a greater power: "But I will show you the one to fear: Fear him who has authority to throw people into hell after death. Yes, I say to you, this is the one to fear!" (Luke 12:5). Yes, they were aware of the dangers they could see, but Jesus points them to a big-picture, greater reality. In his paraphrase in *The Message*, pastor Eugene Peterson puts it like this: "I'm speaking to you as dear friends. Don't be bluffed into silence or insincerity by the threats of religious bullies. True, they can kill you, but *then* what can they do? There's nothing they can do to your soul, your core being. Save your fear for God, who holds your entire life—body and soul—in his hands."[2]

> You can fear God and know that you have an infinite value to God, since He protected you at the expense of Jesus' very life.

Of course, in Jesus they are reconciled and have forgiveness and peace with God, so they actually become safe in the hands of the One they rightly fear: "Jesus asserts that, in hostile situations of life imperilment, God is the only one who should be feared, but the character of God is such that one need not fear him!"[3] Jesus wants His "dear friends" to remember there is more to life than what they can see right in front of them. As His dear friend, you can fear God and know that you have an infinite value to God, since He protected you at the expense of Jesus' very life.

BIRDS AND HAIR

Jesus makes sure His friends understand how much God cares for them. "Aren't five sparrows sold for two pennies? Yet not one of them is forgotten in God's sight," He tells them. "Indeed, the hairs of your head are all counted. Don't be afraid; you are worth more than many sparrows" (Luke 12:6–7).

During COVID, I acquired a set of birds. A friend with four parakeets decided that four was two too many. When she asked if I wanted them, I made an uncharacteristic decision (I blame the pandemic stay-at-home orders!)—I said yes. So now I have two little birds, one green and one blue, that chatter in their cage for the majority of the day. I can hear their tweeting from my living room, and reading about sparrows reminds me that God hasn't forgotten my little birds either. He knows about my tiny friends (unoriginally named Blue and Green). They bring me joy as they fly around their cage, playing with the toys I buy them and making their sweet (okay, sometimes annoying) sounds, too. Naturally, I am fond of them. But imagine! God notices not only my little birds, but the whole of creation. This truth lies beyond my own understanding.

Jesus makes His persuasive argument based on this great love and understanding of the Father, basically saying, "If God cares for the little birds of His creation, how much more does He care for you? You are the crown jewel of all of creation. Believe He cares for you." Often when we are afraid, we also feel forgotten or unseen. You are not forgotten. Every time you see a bird, remember that beautiful truth about the Lord's pervasive care.

Jesus goes on to tell the disciples that not only are they seen, but they are seen individually and intimately: "Indeed, the hairs of your head are all counted. Don't be afraid; you are worth more than many sparrows" (Luke 12:7). Richard Lenski writes about why Jesus used what seemed like insignificant examples, sparrows and hairs:

> The sparrows fly over our heads, the hairs of our head are a part of us and vastly smaller and individually quite insignificant. The human head has about 140,000 hairs. Jesus says that each hair is not only counted as one but has its own individual number and is thus individually known and distinguished. So if any one hair is removed, God knows precisely which one it is (21:18; Acts 27:34). These two illustrations exemplify the infinite extent of God's provident care. The smaller the objects are in our eyes, and the less the value, the greater is the force of the argument when God's own children are now mentioned.[4]

You are known—so intimately known that God knows the hairs on your head. Every single time you see one of your hairs fall onto your shirt or you see one on your pillow, remember that God sees it too. He even counts that hair. That is how dedicated He is to taking care of you, body and soul.

Fearful one, God sees you. He doesn't see you in some detached, unconcerned way. He sees you and cares for you. He values you. Jesus doesn't diminish the danger you may be in, but instead calls you to look to a truer reality: the reality that you are loved, that your very soul has been saved because of the work He has done for you and in your place. When you are fearful, hear Jesus call you His friend. Look for birds, look for hairs, look for the ordinary ways He shows you that He knows your struggle and is standing beside you in it. You don't have a Savior who doesn't understand physical danger. You don't have a Savior who asks you to do something He would never do. You have a Savior who spoke truth to the religious elite and understood the cost. He bears that cost with you. Remember the birds.

eight

JESUS WITH THE FORGOTTEN

It was always the plan that in the midst of the catastrophic brokenness
in this world, grace would surprise us all.

ALIA JOY

"Truly I tell you, whatever you did for one of the least of these brothers
and sisters of mine, you did for me."

MATTHEW 25:40

Have you ever felt invisible? Maybe you were on the periphery of a group—and not one person drew you into conversation. Maybe the work of others in your department gets noticed, while you fail to get promoted. Maybe you have a sibling or best friend who just shines—and, without meaning to, that person leaves you feeling like you're in the shadows. We've all had the experience of feeling sidelined—if not completely forgotten.

You've been spending enough time in the Gospels lately to realize that Jesus tended to champion the people society pushed to the sidelines. Jesus instructed His disciples to let the children come to Him. He routinely drew long lines of the sick, weak, demon-possessed, and disabled. He valued and befriended women. He shocked the local religious establishment by bothering to know prostitutes, tax collectors, and other "sinners." Obviously, Jesus had a different way of seeing the people around Him than we humans naturally do.

We might have our eyes open, but can we truly see people? C. S. Lewis wrote about the people that we meet—and who they really are:

> It is a serious thing to live in a society of possible gods and
> goddesses, to remember that the dullest, most uninteresting
> person you can talk to may one day be a creature which, if
> you saw it now, you would be strongly tempted to worship,
> or else a horror and a corruption such as you now meet, if at
> all, only in a nightmare. All day long we are, in some degree,
> helping each other to one or the other of these destinations.
> It is in the light of these overwhelming possibilities, it is
> with the awe and the circumspection proper to them, that
> we should conduct all of our dealings with one another,
> all friendships, all loves, all play, all politics. There are no
> ordinary people. You have never talked to a mere mortal.
> Nations, cultures, arts, civilizations—these are mortal, and
> their life is to ours as the life of a gnat. But it is immortals
> whom we joke with, work with, marry, snub, and exploit—
> immortal horrors or everlasting splendors.[1]

What Mr. Lewis is getting at is that if we really saw people, truly saw them as the image bearers of God—immortal beings who will spend eternity either glorified and with the Lord or separated from God forever—we would treat them differently. If every time you looked at others you saw them correctly with their true value, you would see how gloriously they represent

> How easily we categorize and other-ize those around us so we don't have to dignify their opinions with any thought or care.

God and be tempted to fall down and worship them. And yet we find it so easy to walk right past a person in the street without even glancing in their direction, or to ignore our children when they call us for the sixth time in a row. How easily we categorize and other-ize those around us so we don't have to dignify their opinions with any thought or care.

We human beings are truly accomplished at ignoring or overlooking others! No wonder so many feel forgotten.

Jesus lived and taught a better way. How did Jesus treat those we feel so comfortable ignoring? How did Jesus see others? Matthew 25 shows that Jesus treats those marginalized people the same way He treats us. When we come to see that we ourselves are often the forgotten ones—that we ourselves are the ones who get ignored or sidelined—when we see ourselves as the "other," we will be changed. Our hearts will grow, and our eyes will be opened to see the "others" we walk by every single day.

PARABLE OF THE SHEEP AND GOATS

Jesus was especially good at telling a story to paint a picture of truth. The book of Matthew particularly contains a lot of the parables Jesus told. Jesus told this parable as one of a set of several that point toward the end times or the final judgment. This discourse takes place near the end of Jesus' life. You can almost hear the urgency in His tone as He is finishing up the teaching part of His ministry. Jesus doesn't want His disciples surprised by what God is asking of them. He wants them to be fully aware of what being a Christ follower means. So, He paints a picture for them by telling a story about His second coming:

> "When the Son of Man comes in his glory, and all the angels with him, then he will sit on his glorious throne. All the nations will be gathered before him, and he will separate them one from another, just as a shepherd separates the sheep from the goats. He will put the sheep on his right and the goats on the left. Then the King will say to those on his right, 'Come, you who are blessed by my Father; inherit the kingdom prepared for you from the foundation of the world.
>
> "'For I was hungry and you gave me something to eat; I was thirsty and you gave me something to drink; I was a stranger and you took me in; I was naked and you clothed me; I was sick and you took care of me; I was in prison and you visited me.'
>
> "Then the righteous will answer him, 'Lord, when did we see you hungry and feed you, or thirsty and give you something to drink? When did we see you a stranger and take you in, or without clothes and clothe you? When did we see you sick, or in prison, and visit you?'
>
> "And the King will answer them, 'Truly I tell you, whatever you did for one of the least of these brothers and sisters of mine, you did for me.'
>
> "Then he will also say to those on the left, 'Depart from me, you who are cursed, into the eternal fire prepared for

the devil and his angels! For I was hungry and you gave me nothing to eat; I was thirsty and you gave me nothing to drink; I was a stranger and you didn't take me in; I was naked and you didn't clothe me, sick and in prison and you didn't take care of me.'

"Then they too will answer, 'Lord, when did we see you hungry, or thirsty, or a stranger, or without clothes, or sick, or in prison, and not help you?'

"Then he will answer them, 'Truly I tell you, whatever you did not do for one of the least of these, you did not do for me.'

"And they will go away into eternal punishment, but the righteous into eternal life." (Matt. 25:31–46)

Jesus starts out with a wondrous picture that includes angels, a glorious throne, and a multicultural multitude gathered before His glory. Then the story gets a twist: Jesus starts separating all the people into two groups, the sheep and the goats. The sheep are the ones who are His, the ones who have trusted in Christ and become children of God. Jesus invites His family into the kingdom, into the everlasting glory that has been prepared for them from eternity past.

JESUS AS THE FORGOTTEN ONE

In Jesus' narration, the Son of Man, this glorious King, says the most astounding thing: "I was hungry and you fed me, I was thirsty and you gave me a drink, I was homeless and you gave me a room, I was shivering and you gave me clothes, I was sick and you stopped to visit, I was in prison and you came to me" (Matt. 25:36 MSG).

This list Jesus describes of needs being met is remarkable; the list really does cover all the most important needs of the human existence:

The first two, hunger and thirst, form a natural pair (basic inner physical needs); and the last two, the sick and prisoners, have in common the prospect of physical isolation. Perhaps the middle two, hospitality and clothing, have in common protection from the elements. The first, second, and fourth items relate to basic survival needs, while the third, fifth, and sixth all deal with things that pose a threat of isolation in one way or another.[2]

It should be noted that the last "I was in prison and you came to me" isn't necessarily just about visiting someone while they were locked up. In this culture the only thing that the prison would provide would be a place of shelter. The prisoner had to rely on the generosity of their friends or family to feed and take care of them. Starvation and death would come to a prisoner without visitors.

The glorious King is commending the righteous for mundane kindnesses in life: feeding some, giving water, giving clothing, taking care of the sick, visiting prisoners. None of these acts require flashy, mountain-moving kind of faith. One commentator observes, "Big miracles aren't happening here; little ministries are."[3] The commonness and yet utter necessity of these deeds is a true testament to the fact that Jesus understood what it felt like to be human. He knew what it was to take on our skin. He knew what it was like to feel hungry, thirsty, cold, isolated, and sick. He knew these deeds, though common, were not unimportant. "Luther somewhere says of this text that every home is a little hospital, where a loving parent performs all the ministries of our text with children, spouse, and extended family."[4] These acts of love are ones we can perform every single day with those around us.

Jesus' sheep—the ones who belong to Him—have, day in and day out, regularly acted in love out of reverence for Christ: "We may be looking at Jesus' favorite people in these simple givers of food and drink (in economic ministries), in providers of clothing and shelter (in social ministries), and in visitors of the sick and shamed (in visitation ministries)."[5]

Meanwhile, the righteous (the sheep) are utterly aghast at this claim by the Son of Man. Can you imagine them wracking their memories trying to figure out when, exactly, they had encountered their King and served Him? Finally, they would come to the end of themselves and have

> **We see how Jesus treats the forgotten. He doesn't just interact with them, He identifies with them.**

to say, "Master, what are you talking about? When did we ever see you hungry and feed you, thirsty and give you a drink? And when did we ever see you sick or in prison and come to you?" (Matt. 25:37–38 MSG). They're each thinking, *I am sure that if I fed or clothed a king, I'd remember it!*

This is the moment when we see how Jesus treats the forgotten. He doesn't just interact with them, He identifies with them: "Then the King will say, 'I'm telling the solemn truth: Whenever you did one of these things to someone overlooked or ignored, that was me—you did it to me'" (vv. 39–40 MSG). Jesus doesn't put Himself into this parable talking about Himself as one of the righteous performing acts of kindness. He identifies with the hungry one, the thirsty one, the homeless or sick one, and the prisoner! Jesus knows. Jesus knows what it is to feel human feelings of need, neglect, and loneliness.

This parable began with a description of God's Son in glory: "When the Son of Man comes in his glory, and all the angels with him, then he will sit on his glorious throne. All the nations will be gathered before him" (v. 31). That glorious King, Jesus—enthroned in power before the nations—identifies as the needy and forgotten. Oh, what beauty, what humility, what love He displays! This is how Jesus lived His whole life on earth. He chose to humble Himself; He chose not to access all of who He was as God incarnate. Instead, He chose to take on the form of a human being with needs.

> **Jesus chose to take on the form of a human being with needs.**

We tend to place the value of our service on the perceived "value" of the person being served. It's one thing for me to give a child a drink, but that same act seems way more meaningful if I give the drink to someone I consider important. But Jesus turns our thinking upside down. Jesus is teaching us that punching a hole in a juice box for a kid is as important as bringing a glass of water to the President. Jesus identifies more with the child than He does with the President, saying, "What you do to the least of these you do to me." Not only should this make us stand in awe at how beautifully upside down the kingdom of heaven is, but it should also help us see the value of the ordinary work we do every single day.

Forgotten one, you aren't forgotten at all. You don't just have a Savior who sees you and knows your needs; you have a Savior who stands next to you and says, "She is Me. I am him." He doesn't mind identifying as the overlooked or ignored. In fact, see how Jesus is described in Isaiah 53:2–3: "He didn't have an impressive form or majesty that we should look at him, no appearance that we should desire him. He was despised and rejected by men, a man of suffering who knew what sickness was. He was like someone people turned away from; he was despised, and we didn't value him." Jesus, the glorious King of heaven, was unvalued— someone people turned away from—and understood suffering and sickness. Nothing in His appearance made Him desirable.

In human terms, Jesus was forgettable—except He wasn't!

Neither are you forgettable. Neither are the people we walk by every day. Jesus identifies with the least and the forgotten. May we have eyes to see the value in all of those around us, including ourselves.

nine

JESUS WITH THOSE IN DANGER

When Jesus stood up, he said to her, "Woman, where are they?
Has no one condemned you?"

"No one, Lord," she answered.

"Neither do I condemn you," said Jesus. "Go, and from now on do
not sin anymore."

JOHN 8:10–11

W hether or not you know what it is to experience true
danger may depend on your socioeconomic status, your
birthplace, or your ethnicity. For some of us, "danger" is something we just watch on the big screen while eating a box of Cheez-
Its. For others, danger is something they face every time they walk

out the front door—or maybe even every time they walk in the front door. There are lives compounded by one perilous difficulty after another, and certainly none of us get through life without encountering a dangerous moment or two. Sometimes troubles come upon us through no fault of our own, and other times we land ourselves in trouble with our own poor decision-making.

We have already seen that Jesus experienced real dangers during His years of ministry. The gospel of John shows us a time when Jesus intervened to rescue a woman whose life was in danger:

> At dawn he went to the temple again, and all the people were coming to him. He sat down and began to teach them.
>
> Then the scribes and the Pharisees brought a woman caught in adultery, making her stand in the center. "Teacher," they said to him, "this woman was caught in the act of committing adultery. In the law Moses commanded us to stone such women. So what do you say?" They asked this to trap him, in order that they might have evidence to accuse him.
>
> Jesus stooped down and started writing on the ground with his finger. When they persisted in questioning him, he stood up and said to them, "The one without sin among you should be the first to throw a stone at her." Then he stooped down again and continued writing on the ground. When they heard this, they left one by one, starting with the older men. Only he was left, with the woman in the center. When Jesus stood up, he said to her, "Woman, where are they? Has no one condemned you?"
>
> "No one, Lord," she answered.
>
> "Neither do I condemn you," said Jesus. "Go, and from now on do not sin anymore." (John 8:2–10)

THE TRAP

The Pharisees were once again out to find a way to trap Jesus. This was a fun little game they played almost every time they interacted with Him. They wanted to discount His credibility. They wanted to make others see Him as a fraud. They wanted to undermine His wisdom. Again and again, they discovered that when you go up against Wisdom embodied, you never walk away a winner.

Again and again, the Pharisees discovered that when you go up against Wisdom embodied, you never walk away a winner.

Make no mistake—the Pharisees didn't bring this woman to Jesus because they cared about her sin or cared about her soul. If they really did care about the law and its demands, they would have brought in the man with whom she'd been caught in the act. Instead, they left the man behind and only brought the woman. They saw her as expendable in their little setup. Her life, her soul, was meaningless to them. These religious leaders were aware of Jesus' reputation for being merciful—and they also knew the penalty for adultery was death. They wanted to stump Him by posing a no-win situation. Commentator Gary Burge writes,

> This is a powerful story because it paints a strong picture of harsh judges who have neglected their responsibility to care for the soul of the woman. She is disposable. Their aim is to corner Jesus, and her life is a tool in their theological gambit to make him either condemn her (thus sacrificing his commitment to grace) or forgive her (thus sacrificing his commitment to God's law).[1]

What will Jesus do?

THE SCENE

Take a minute to set the scene in your mind. Especially when we have heard these stories from God's Word several times, it's easy to forget that these are real people and real situations. Take yourself to Jerusalem. Go to the temple. Picture Jesus coming in and sitting down to teach. See the crowd gather around this rabbi, and feel their building anticipation for what He was going to say.

At that moment the Pharisees crash the party with a woman in tow. The Scriptures make a point to let you know they make her "stand in the center." They want her humiliation to be complete. They want everyone there to see and to hear what is about to happen. They are confident they have Jesus exactly where they want Him. They bait their trap: "This woman was caught in the act of committing adultery. In the law, Moses commanded us to stone such women. So what do you say?"

These men are misquoting the law—in much the same way the snake, the accuser, did in the garden of Eden. Genesis 3 records how God told Adam and Even not to eat of the tree of the knowledge of good and evil, but the serpent changes God's command to "not to touch or eat of the tree of the knowledge of good and evil." The accusers of this woman caught in adultery say, "Moses commanded us to stone such women." What Moses truly commanded was that both parties be put to death.

Leave it to Jesus to do the most surprising, most unlikely thing.

These men intended to use the law to kill this woman. Her life was over. She was in danger. Though these men are wielding power that has compounded her danger, this woman's own sinful choices got her started toward peril—which makes Jesus' response all the more fascinating.

THE STOOP

Leave it to Jesus to do the most surprising, most unlikely thing. Jesus stoops down and starts writing in the sand. We have no way of knowing what He was writing, and I am not sure it is helpful to make guesses as to what He was doing. The scholar Bruner attempts an explanation:

> I think it likely that Jesus' stooping to write on the ground served, at least, to draw the crowd's accusing looks from the woman. I think Jesus may also be taking his time in order not to dignify the question by a too prompt or a too defensive response. He may also be intentionally adding drama to the occasion. (He might even be buying time to think for a moment about how to answer this trap question. This possibility takes Jesus' true humanity seriously.)[2]

This act of stooping and doodling infuriates the religious even more. The accusers think Jesus is stalling, so they "persist in questioning him." They want an answer, and they want it now. Finally, Jesus gives them an answer. His one sentence stops their self-righteous momentum: "The one without sin among you should be the first to throw a stone at her."

Jesus demolishes their trap with a devastating blow. Jesus acknowledges the law of Moses but draws their attention to the fact that not one of them has ever followed the law perfectly. Then Jesus goes back to His drawing. Bruner again draws our attention to the compassion of Christ:

It's the loving nature of Jesus to protect. Here Jesus takes the gaze of shame; soon He would take the whole punishment for sin.

When Jesus a second time "stooped down again and was writing some more on the ground," after asking his incriminating question, the redundance suggests that Jesus may now be trying to avert the crowd's critical attention from the accused's *accusers* and from their shame, just as he had earlier sought to protect the woman from her shame and shamers. Jesus is the consummate protector of persons— even now the person of his attackers.[3]

It's the loving nature of Jesus to protect—first deflecting harsh attention from the accused woman and then deflecting it again from the accusers. Here Jesus takes the gaze of shame; soon He would take the whole punishment for sin.

THE DEPARTURE

And so, each of these accusers walk away. The older and then the younger, they turn and leave. They are confronted with their own brokenness. They can't cast the first stone; they are not without sin. "This remarkable response was perhaps silent acknowledgment that in many ways they were no better than her," writes Colin Kruse. "In the end everyone had departed: the crowd, the teachers of the law and the Pharisees. Now 'only Jesus was left, with the woman still standing there' where she had been placed by her accusers."[4]

> Jesus understands the price we must pay when we stand up for the upside-down kingdom of God.

There was only One standing in the temple who was without sin. Only One could have thrown the stone and administered the deserved judgment. The sinless One is the One who chose, once for always, not to administer the deserved judgment. That One would become sin for us all so that we might become the righteousness of God (2 Cor. 5:21). That One would take our punishment, our deserved judgment, and instead give us His own deserved reward for a life lived sinlessly.

THE PROCLAMATION

The accusers have left this woman alone with Jesus—a woman discovered alone with a man in a terrible situation ends up presented to another man. But this Man knows her. This Man loves her. This Man would never use her. This Man protects her. The Great Forgiver says to her, "Woman, where are they? Has no one condemned you?"

She can answer this Man safely: "No one, Lord."

> Jesus doesn't just offer forgiveness. He offers a new way of life.

Jesus forgives her: "Neither do I condemn you," He tells her. "Go, and from now on do not sin anymore."

The only One who could condemn her chooses to save instead. Jesus takes this woman in danger away from the brink of death and ushers her into real life. He doesn't just offer forgiveness; He offers a new way of life: "Go, and from now on do not sin anymore." His love and forgiveness move her into a life worth living. The law only had the power to kill. The gospel has the power to restore, revive, and remake this woman.

The forgiveness of Christ is offered just as freely to those accusers—those people who thought they hadn't done much wrong themselves, those who didn't feel the weight of their own sin, those who reveled in the downfall of another sinner.

Both the accused woman and her accusers were in different kinds of danger. We all know how quick we are to justify our own actions or to take our own sin lightly. Each of us may need to be confronted with the desperateness of our own situation.

Christ's forgiveness in each of our lives diminishes as we lose touch with the depth of our own sinfulness. When we no longer see ourselves in the drama of the woman, when we feel we are free from accusation and judgment, we lose sight of God's grace. Jesus is not simply committed to the requirements of the law, but to the care and transformation of the woman before him—and every person who likewise brings a debt of sin into the circle where he sits. This drama of Jesus and the woman gains power when I become that woman and reflect on the seriousness of my own jeopardy. Through this new vision, I gain a new glimpse of Jesus' love and mercy.[5]

If you are in danger, maybe even because of your own sin, Jesus offers you new life. He offers you protection and pardon. He offers you Himself. The only way we get the protection and the pardon is if Jesus puts Himself in danger in our place. He did that willingly for this woman, and He does that willingly for you and for me. He never asks us to downplay the danger we experience, but He does ask us to see Him there with us. You may have real reason to be afraid, but you also have real reason to feel cared for. He sees you. He isn't ashamed of you. He longs to protect you from any injustice you may face. There is a better way to live. There is a better Man to love us.

ten

JESUS WITH THOSE WHO NEED HEALING

Moved with compassion, Jesus reached out his hand and touched him.
"I am willing," he told him. "Be made clean."

MARK 1:41

There isn't an area of our lives that isn't touched by sin in some way or another. We know that wherever sin goes, brokenness is sure to be the result. We are broken mentally, physically, spiritually, sexually. We know this is true because in every area of our lives we must fight against selfishness. We must fight against pushing forward our own agenda and what profits us. We know this because the Bible tells us sin infects every aspect of our world and being. We know this because each of us can think of ways we do not operate the way we should. As Augustine, the church father and philosopher, wrote, man "turns away from God to himself."[1] This turning in on ourselves causes us to sin against others and others to sin against us.

Since every area of our lives is broken by sin, it follows that every area of our lives needs healing from the Healer. Our focus will be on those who need physical healing and spiritual healing, and we'll discover that in many cases the brokenness we live with day by day has not been brought about by any actions of our own but simply because we live in a broken world and encounter broken people.

In this broken world, things are not as they should be. How does Jesus confront that fact, and how does He bring healing?

SPIRITUAL HEALING

The gospel of Mark unfolds a dramatic story of Jesus encountering spiritual evil—evil that was tormenting the life of a young man.

> They came to the other side of the sea, to the region of the Gerasenes. As soon as he got out of the boat, a man with an unclean spirit came out of the tombs and met him. He lived in the tombs, and no one was able to restrain him anymore—not even with a chain—because he often had been bound with shackles and chains, but had torn the chains apart and smashed the shackles. No one was strong enough to subdue him. Night and day among the tombs and on the mountains, he was always crying out and cutting himself with stones.
>
> When he saw Jesus from a distance, he ran and knelt down before him. And he cried out with a loud voice,

"What do you have to do with me, Jesus, Son of the Most High God? I beg you before God, don't torment me!" For he had told him, "Come out of the man, you unclean spirit!"

"What is your name?" he asked him.

"My name is Legion," he answered him, "because we are many." And he begged him earnestly not to send them out of the region.

A large herd of pigs was there, feeding on the hillside. The demons begged him, "Send us to the pigs, so that we may enter them." So he gave them permission, and the unclean spirits came out and entered the pigs. The herd of about two thousand rushed down the steep bank into the sea and drowned there.

The men who tended them ran off and reported it in the town and the countryside, and people went to see what had happened. They came to Jesus and saw the man who had been demon-possessed, sitting there, dressed and in his right mind; and they were afraid. Those who had seen it described to them what had happened to the demon-possessed man and told about the pigs. Then they began to beg him to leave their region.

As he was getting into the boat, the man who had been demon-possessed begged him earnestly that he might remain with him. Jesus did not let him but told him, "Go home to your own people, and report to them how much the Lord has done for you and how he has had mercy on you." (Mark 5:1–19)

Mark describes a situation that is wild and fairly unfamiliar to us today. Because evil spirits had taken over a man, he lived like a wild man, alone in the tombs, and unrestrainable. He couldn't

The wild man instantly saw what others could not—that Jesus was the "Son of the Most High God."

be chained or held back. He was constantly cutting himself, and he continually shrieked with the agony of his torment. He was a disturbed man, and that was apparent to everyone in the area.

Scholar David Garland draws the parallel of this one man's disturbance with the dangerous brokenness of all humankind:

> No one had the strength to "subdue" him. The Greek word used here (*damazo*) is used for taming a wild animal and is better translated, "no one was able to *tame* him." Obviously this demoniac roams free because all attempts to constrain him have failed. . . . One does not normally "tame" human beings; one tames wild animals (or the tongue, James 3:8). People treat him like a wild animal, and he acts like one.
>
> He is banished as an outcast from society and must dwell with those whose sleep will not be disturbed by his shrieks echoing through the night as he lacerates his body with stones. He is a microcosm of the whole of creation, inarticulately groaning for redemption (Rom. 8:22). He is condemned to live out his days alone amid the decaying bones of the dead, with no one who loves him and no one to love. Malignant spirits always deface humanity and destroy life.[2]

This demon-possessed man, who spent most of his waking hours operating in some sort of reality all its own, suddenly experiences true clarity when Jesus comes near. When he saw Jesus, "he ran to him and knelt down" and "he cried out with a loud voice." He asked Jesus what He wanted with him. Somehow the demons tormenting this wild man instantly saw what others could not; he names Jesus as the "Son of the Most High God." He begs Jesus not to torment him, obviously aware of the power Jesus possessed. Garland comments: "Unlike humans, who cannot quite fathom the reality of the divine breaking into human history (4:41), evil spirits always recognize Jesus' divine origin (1:24; 3:11; see James 2:19) and quake in his presence. They know that they are pitted against vastly superior firepower."[3] This unrestrainable wild man knelt and begged, knowing he was completely outmatched.

HOG WILD

Jesus commands the unclean spirits to come out of the man. When the voice of Legion begs to be allowed to enter a nearby herd of pigs, Jesus obliges the request. This did not end well for the pigs, who rushed straight into the sea and drowned. It's definitely a weird story!

The neighbors reacted badly as well. They were angry about the loss of the livestock. But strangely, they were terrified by the sight of the former wild man, dressed and clean and in his right mind. One could say this community's priorities were a bit skewed. But this demonstration of Jesus' power frightened them—and they wanted Him gone. They didn't want any more of what He was offering.

> **Jesus had looked beyond the filth, wounds, bad smells, and erratic behavior and saw straight into his humanity.**

The power of Christ's love unsettled them:

> They are more comfortable with the malevolent forces that take captive human beings and destroy animals than they are with the one who can expel them. They can cope with the odd demon-possessed wild man who terrorizes the neighborhood with random acts of violence. But they want to keep someone with Jesus' power at lake's length—on

the other side of the sea. They must consider Jesus more dangerous and worrisome than the demons.[4]

START SPREADING THE NEWS

Fully restored and in his right mind, the formerly demon-possessed man wanted to follow Jesus. And no wonder! Jesus had looked beyond the filth, wounds, bad smells, and erratic behavior and saw straight into his humanity. With one sentence Jesus healed and restored his broken life. Jesus quite literally gave this man his life back.

It was much more typical for Jesus to tell those He'd healed to keep it quiet, but Jesus does something curious here. He tells this healed man, "Go home to your own people, and report to them how much the Lord has done for you and how He had mercy on you." Jesus turns this man into an evangelist, a bearer of the good news of salvation in Jesus. Look closely at what Jesus asks him to report, which provides insight into how Jesus interacts with those who need healing spiritually. Jesus says to testify about all that the Lord has done and the mercy this man was shown.

Jesus asked this man to go do what he had been created to do: find his people and tell them about Jesus.

Jesus works for, with, and in the spiritually broken. He shows mercy to those who need spiritual healing. Jesus didn't want this man to go out and just talk about how much better he was doing. Jesus wanted the man to tell his people that the Lord worked this miracle, that the Lord saw him, loved him, and delivered him. Jesus wanted this man who had been alienated from people and isolated to go find community and share his experience. Jesus restored this broken man and asked him to go do what he had been created to do: find his people and tell them about Jesus. Jesus wanted this man to proclaim that the reversal of darkness was taking place and it had happened in him. Jesus was restoring what had been lost.

PHYSICAL HEALING

The gospel of Mark also contains a short narrative about a man who needed healing in his body:

> Then a man with leprosy came to him and, on his knees, begged him, "If you are willing, you can make me clean." Moved with compassion, Jesus reached out his hand and touched him. "I am willing," he told him. "Be made clean." Immediately the leprosy left him, and he was made clean. Then he sternly warned him and sent him away at once, telling him, "See that you say nothing to anyone; but go and show yourself to the priest, and offer what Moses commanded for your cleansing, as a testimony to them." Yet he went out and began to proclaim it widely and to spread the news, with the result that Jesus could no longer enter a town openly. But he was out in deserted places, and they came to him from everywhere. (Mark 1:40–45)

Like the wild man oppressed by demons, this man with leprosy comes to Jesus, believing He had the power to bring the change he needed—healing from leprosy. This physical disease made him an outcast, as he was not permitted to be around anyone who didn't also suffer from leprosy. He would have been removed from his community and his family and placed in isolation. So while the more obvious affliction was this terribly painful

His suffering was so intense, he was willing to break the law in order to come close to Jesus.

bacterial infection, this man also suffered from the mental and emotional pain of enduring it alone.

The desperateness of his situation makes him willing to break the law in order to come close to Jesus. His suffering was so intense, he was willing to endure the consequences of breaking those ceremonial laws.

He approaches Jesus. He kneels. He begs, "If you are willing, you can make me clean."

The ball is in Jesus' court. The man has made his plea. He has taken his shot. He waits. What was probably seconds must feel like an eternity as he waits with anticipation to see what Jesus will do. How will Jesus interact with this man who is visibly repulsive, unclean, and an outcast?

MOVED WITH COMPASSION

There is a bit of discussion about how the Greek word *orgízō* is translated here. The word that is translated "compassion" in the Greek actually meant "enraged." Why would the original text say Jesus was enraged at this man's request? R. T. France shares this insight:

> The most likely explanation is, perhaps, that the suffering caused by the disease, both physically and socially, moved Jesus not only to compassion but to anger at the presence of such evil in the world; perhaps also over the insensitivity of the social taboo. That the anger was not directed against the man himself is implied by the immediate compassionate response."[5]

Jesus' compassion toward the man includes righteous anger at the wrong being done to him. Jesus' emotions don't just stay

feelings; they nearly always lead to an action. The enraged compassion He feels moves Him toward this sufferer. Jesus joins this
lawbreaker in his disregard of the rules.

Jesus reaches out His hand and touches him. "I am willing. Be
made clean."

Immediately the man is clean.

Alan Cole sees Jesus coming straight into the suffering and
stench, for the sake of taking it upon Himself:

> Wherever the compassionate Christ and the yearning
> sinner meet, there then comes instantaneous and complete
> cleansing. In the antiseptic cleanliness of modern hospitals,
> we lose sight of the wonder of the parable of Jesus in all his
> purity stooping to touch the ugliness and stench of our sin
> to bring healing and forgiveness. In the ancient world, the
> attitude toward leprosy was not unlike the popular attitude
> to suspected sufferers from AIDS today. To the pious Jew,
> conscious of the ritual uncleanness of the leper (Lev. 13:3),
> the wonder became even more staggering: Jesus was will-
> ing to incur defilement (as they saw it), so that the defiled
> leper might be made clean. The whole of the gospel is here
> in a nutshell: Christ redeems us from the curse by becom-
> ing under a curse for our sake (Gal. 3:13).[6]

Our compassionate Jesus sees sufferers and desires not only
to alleviate physical suffering but emotional
and mental suffering as well. Jesus touches
this man. Make no mistake, this was probably the first physical touch this man had received in a very long time.

Jesus' care extended to this man's spiritual
well-being. David Garland explains,

**We are known and
loved. Jesus cares for
every single aspect of
who we are.**

In the time of Jesus, leprosy was viewed as the classic punishment for sin. It was the telltale sign that the sufferer was a culprit who had committed sins unknown to his neighbors. The suffering indicated that while sin might be hidden from others, it could not be hidden from God, and it served as forewarning of the ultimate fate of the sinner.[7]

Jesus doesn't just see us as a body, or as a soul, or as an emotional being. We are known and loved. Jesus cares for every single aspect of who we are.

Jesus gives the healed man strict instructions not to go around telling everyone what had happened, but instead to go straight to the priest. The priest would be the one who could pronounce that this man was clean—disease-free. Jesus wanted this man restored to fellowship, to be welcomed back into the community.

Dear ones in need of healing, Jesus sees you. While others may turn away, while you may be ostracized, Jesus draws close. During your physical suffering, never doubt that you have a Savior who has suffered physically and understands your pain. During your emotional suffering, never doubt that you have a Healer who feels compassion and works for your good in every situation. While your physical, emotional, and spiritual suffering may never be completely healed during your lifetime, there is an unstoppable reality coming toward you. One day you will experience complete healing. That day may seem like a faint hope slow to materialize, but you can look at the way Jesus loved the sufferer and believe that He loves you. What God promises will take place. He is willing. You will be made whole.

eleven

JESUS WITH THOSE IN NEED

*"I have compassion on the crowd, because they've already stayed
with me three days and have nothing to eat."*

MARK 8:2

I have incredibly curly hair. I didn't always though. I had stick
straight hair until I was about twelve, when hormones started
kicking in. Within about a year, my hair was curly. Weird, I know.
My hair is so curly that I only brush it about twice a week. When
I do brush it, great clumps of hair come out on the brush. Don't
worry! I'm not going bald. The average person loses about a hundred hairs per day. For me, these loose hairs stay close to my head,

trapped in my curls, and don't fall to the ground. Brushing brings them all out.

Jesus is paying attention even to things we may consider inconsequential. He cares about our needs.

For years, I had no idea what to do with my own curly hair, so I tend to go on about it. If you ever need curly advice, I'm your girl. But the real reason I mention my hair is the amazing truth that God knows every single hair on my head—and on yours. Luke 12 reports Jesus' teaching about how God cares for us and every need and detail of our lives. He pays attention to things in our lives we don't even know are happening. I may have a bunch of loose hairs without realizing they are no longer attached, but God knows.

Jesus' point is the one I'm trying to make. If God cares about hairs, He cares so much more about our hearts, souls, and minds. He is paying attention even to things we may consider inconsequential. Jesus cares about our needs.

THE FIRST MIRACLE

The very first recorded miracle performed by Jesus had to do with a family in need. John 2:1–3 sets the stage: "On the third day a wedding took place in Cana of Galilee. Jesus' mother was there, and Jesus and his disciples were invited to the wedding as well. When the wine ran out, Jesus' mother told him, 'They don't have any wine.'"

Jesus was at a wedding! Stop for a moment to recognize that Jesus did the normal things that families and friends do. His divinity didn't stop Him from going to a weeklong party to rejoice with His friends because of the love they had for each other and to celebrate their commitment to each other. Jesus had begun His ministry, but His kingdom work included being with friends and family, rejoicing in the beauty of love, drinking good wine, and eating good food. His participation in this wedding elevates the eternal worth of enjoying a good party.

Now back to the miracle. In our culture we don't understand the serious implications of wine running out at a wedding. During Jesus' time, running out of wine at a wedding would have been considered a huge social blunder. "This is not merely an embarrassing situation," writes Gary Burge, "it is a dishonoring crisis for the host."[1] The lack of wine would have ruined the wedding as well as the host's reputation.

At first Jesus seems to be offended by the fact that His mother has come to tell Him about the wine situation. "'What has this concern of yours to do with me, woman?' Jesus asked. 'My hour has not yet come'" (John 2:4). While the language may seem disrespectful to us, most scholars believe Jesus was just reminding Mary that He wasn't there to do her bidding but rather to obey His Father. I must say that I love Mary's response: "'Do whatever he tells you,' his mother told the servants" (v. 5). She basically responded by saying, "Cool, cool, cool. Servers, just do what He asks you to do. Let's get the wine flowing again."

> "Fill the jars with water," Jesus told them. So they filled them to the brim. Then he said to them, "Now draw some out and take it to the headwaiter." And they did.
>
> When the headwaiter tasted the water (after it had become wine), he did not know where it came from—though the servants who had drawn the water knew. He called the groom and told him, "Everyone sets out the fine wine first, then, after people are drunk, the inferior. But you have kept the fine wine until now." (John 2:7–10)

The surprising beauty of this miracle is that Jesus doesn't do anything halfway. He "goes big or goes home," as the saying goes. Jesus didn't just change the water into wine. Since it's from the hands of Jesus, we can assume it was the best wine they'd ever had! Think of the joy He felt as they tasted the wine, knowing they would be blown away by its superiority. Jesus didn't look at the situation and say, "Your reputation shouldn't matter so much to you. Let's just be grateful for the wine we had and move on." Nope, not our Savior. He cared about what the wedding hosts cared about. He cared about the quality of the party. He cared about their reputation. He cared about something we would consider a superfluous extra. This attention to detail demonstrates a "counting the hairs on your head" level of care.

Jesus didn't just change the water into wine. Since it's from the hands of Jesus, we can assume it was the best wine they'd ever had!

COMPASSION ON THE CROWD

What motivates Christ's heart to provide for His people? We see the answer in Mark 8: "In those days there was again a large crowd, and they had nothing to eat. He called the disciples and said to them, 'I have compassion on the crowd, because they've already stayed with me three days and have nothing to eat. If I send them home hungry, they will collapse on the way, and some of them have come a long distance'" (vv. 1–3). This is the story of Jesus feeding the four thousand. It is the second time Jesus has performed a miracle of this sort. In the gospel of John, we read how Jesus feeds five thousand men plus women and children with only two fish and five loaves of bread.

The practicality of Christ's care for those following Him is exemplified in this passage. He looks around, seeing that there is a bunch of people and that there was no food. He feels compassion. Alan Cole writes about Jesus stepping in to meet an everyday need like hunger:

> There is a tendency today to spiritualize the miracles so much that we lose sight of their primary meaning, which is that, when Jesus saw anyone cold, hungry, ill or in distress, his heart went out to them in love and pity (verse 2). In other words, although the miracles of Jesus were certainly used as "signs" to point a spiritual message, the recipient was not made merely a spiritual "stalking-horse." The root of all ministry, whether physical or spiritual, is this genuine inner constraint, which the New Testament writers unanimously see as the love of Christ, at work in us (2 Cor. 5:14).[2]

We need to understand the depth of the feeling Jesus refers to by saying He has "compassion" on the crowd. He wasn't just expressing a nonchalant, weak type of emotion. The word in the Greek conveys gut-wrenching emotion. Jesus really felt for them. He didn't want to send them away to get food because they were out in the middle of nowhere and they wouldn't have made it to food without fainting.

Jesus' care extended past what was expected and beyond those He might be expected to care for.

The first time that Jesus multiplied food was for the Jewish community. This time, commentators agree, the location of the miracle indicates that this time Christ probably fed a group predominantly made up of Gentiles. Jesus reaches out to the people not typically included by the Jewish community. He cared for the physical needs of the ones who were outcasts according to His tradition. His care extended past what was expected and beyond those He might be expected to care for.

James Edwards expounds on this idea:

> There is a lesson here for the people of God in every age, that its enemies are neither forsaken by God nor beyond the compassion of Jesus. On the contrary, the Gentiles, like others "a long distance" away, are the objects of Jesus' compassion. The difference between the Jews' response to the Gentiles and Jesus' response can be seen in Mark's concluding phrase, "And [Jesus] sent them away." The Greek word for "send away," *apolyein*, can mean either "to dismiss" or "get rid of"; or "to release" or "liberate." The first is the Jewish response; the second is Jesus' response, who satisfies the hungry outcasts and liberates them.[3]

THE GREATEST NEED

Jesus never minimized physical needs, but He didn't just stop there. He provided for our greatest need. Turning the water into wine symbolizes the truth that the gospel is greater than anything we have ever known.[4] Jesus provides for us forgiveness and righteousness. His life, death, and resurrection fulfill what we need desperately.

Matthew 6:31–33 records this teaching of Jesus: "So do not worry, saying, 'What shall we eat?' or 'What shall we drink?' or 'What shall we wear?' For the pagans run after all these things, and your heavenly Father knows that you need

Jesus loves to do more than we can ask or imagine.

them. But seek first his kingdom and his righteousness, and all these things will be given to you as well" (NIV). The Great Provider knows your needs. Jesus knew the needs of those around Him, and He worked for their good. He doesn't trivialize these physical needs of provision, but He does call you to recognize that life is more than just the physical. True life lies in the righteousness Christ provided for us.

Needy one, take your desires to Christ. He loves to do more than we can ask or imagine—He has *already* done more than we can ask or imagine. Know that if He doesn't provide in the way you expected or hoped, He has compassion on you and will give you exactly what you need.

twelve

JESUS WITH
THE DEAD

Celebrate the life by all means, but face up to the death of that life. Weep all
the tears you have in you to weep, because whatever may happen next,
if anything does, this has happened. Something precious and irreplaceable
has come to an end and something in you has come to an end with it.
FREDERICK BUECHNER

Jesus wept.
JOHN 11:35

When Jesus came into contact with death, He took action. This makes sense since Jesus' ministry was completely focused on matters of life and death. His ultimate purpose was to bring people new life—which He accomplished by dying Himself and being resurrected three days later in complete demonstration of His power to give life. Throughout the gospel narratives, Jesus is leading people to new life. When Jesus was next to the thief on the cross, Jesus didn't save him from physical death. But He did promise paradise and an eternity with Him (Luke 23:43).

Death has been all around us in recent years, with the coronavirus pandemic taking a cruel toll. For me, the sad news of the COVID death of a well-loved local pastor of a large church has recently rocked the Christian community around San Diego. So many friends are telling how they first learned about loving the Bible from this man. Part of the post announcing this sad loss said, "We are all in shock and heartbroken. We find comfort in knowing that he is rejoicing in heaven with his beloved Jesus." In the face of death, we try to make sense of it and to find comfort, even while we are grieving the loss. Life feels so tenuous and uncertain, but one thing we know for sure: for the believer, death never has the final word.

Only Jesus could encounter death and be able to reverse it, and the gospel writers took care to include three times when Jesus encountered death and did choose to reverse it, giving each of these people, who of course would eventually end up dying, a future in which they could be raised to new life.

FROM FUNERAL PROCESSION TO STREET PARTY

The book of Luke has been describing how Jesus, with His traveling band of disciples, travels from town to town, teaching and performing great miracles. As the travelers are heading toward the town of Nain, themselves a group full of life and joy, they encounter a mournful group of people grieving a death:

> Afterward he was on his way to a town called Nain. His disciples and a large crowd were traveling with him. Just as he

neared the gate of the town, a dead man was being carried out. He was his mother's only son, and she was a widow. A large crowd from the town was also with her. When the Lord saw her, he had compassion on her and said, "Don't weep." Then he came up and touched the open coffin, and the pallbearers stopped. And he said, "Young man, I tell you, get up!"

The dead man sat up and began to speak, and Jesus gave him to his mother. (Luke 7:11–17)

The culture of Jesus' time placed great importance on mourning and attending funerals. Family, friends, and community came together, and grieving was a public practice. In fact, if the family of the deceased knew enough people were not going to attend the funeral, they would hire professional wailers to come and grieve the passing of their loved one. So, when Jesus and His followers encountered this funeral procession, they weren't coming upon a group of people just walking silently down the street "being respectful" like one "should be" at a funeral. These people were letting loose, crying, and lamenting loudly.

To make the matter even more desperate, the chief mourner is a widow about to bury her son, her only son. Emotionally, her devastation was thorough, first burying a husband and then a son. But the loss projected social and financial devastation to come. At this time, in this culture, for a woman not to have a man to provide for the family would have made her destitute. She carried the sad knowledge that the family line would not carry on through her. The situation is so dark, so grave—and then down the street comes Life itself.

When the Lord sees this mother, He has compassion on her. This word *compassion* is one we have already encountered. The word carries a connotation of righteous anger as well as loving empathy. Jesus sees this woman, knows the desperateness of her situation, and has compassion on her. He is angry at death. He looks at the woman and says, "Don't weep." How absurd that sentence must have seemed to her and to those around her! How could she not weep? How could she not be utterly heartbroken? How could she, in this moment that was made for grieving, stop her own heartbreak? James Edwards, who wrote about the transformation of this funeral procession into a street party, says, "Jesus now illustrates how he as the Lord of life is the true fulfillment of his commandments, for he will turn the widow's mourning into laughter."[1]

Jesus does the unthinkable. He touches the open coffin. Again, as contemporary people, we can't register how radical this action was. For the Jews of Jesus' time, touching a coffin meant becoming ritually unclean. Yet Jesus is never afraid to come near to or touch anything that would make Him unclean. The purity in Him conquers any uncleanness. The life that overflows from Christ overcomes the death that had taken this young man.

Then Jesus gives the second command of this encounter: "Young man, I tell you, get up!" If the sorrowing mother hadn't already been able to obey Jesus' first command of "Don't weep," her astonishment at this command would've done the trick. The dead young man sits up and begins to speak! I can only imagine the story he had to tell.

I am a mother of sons, so what Jesus does next is particularly touching to me: "Jesus gave him to his mother." The miracle wasn't finished until the two were reunited. Jesus wasn't just performing a miraculous resurrection as a way to flex His power. He wanted this mother to be comforted. He wanted the son to be restored. Richard Lenski writes, "He himself united mother and son in their nameless joy. 'He gave'—and such a gift—and how he loves to do such giving!"[2]

TALITHA KOUM!

Our next story also involves a parent and a child, but this time Jesus encounters a father and daughter:

> When Jesus had crossed over again by boat to the other side, a large crowd gathered around him while he was by the sea. One of the synagogue leaders, named Jairus, came, and when he saw Jesus, he fell at his feet and begged him earnestly, "My little daughter is dying. Come and lay your hands on her so that she can get well and live." So Jesus went with him, and a large crowd was following and pressing against him. (Mark 5:21–24)

Remember how, in general, the antagonistic Jewish religious leaders were attempting to derail or stifle Jesus' ministry? Yet here comes Jairus, a synagogue leader: "One should also note that Jairus is a member of the Jewish establishment that seems on the whole to be hostile to Jesus. His rank as a leader in a hostile institution does not disqualify him from Jesus' care because he is willing to lay aside whatever social status he has by humbling himself before Jesus in a desperate plea for help."[3] This is a desperate father, and Jesus agrees to go with Jairus.

> Jesus came for everyone. Class, cleanliness, social status, gender, age, perceived importance of need— none of this makes a difference to Christ.

While on their way to Jairus's house, Jesus is stopped by a woman who touched His robe so that she could experience healing. This "interruption" isn't superfluous. Not only does it serve to heal this woman, it provides a clean picture of the truth that Jesus came for everyone—from a synagogue leader to an unclean woman who had been hemorrhaging for twelve years. Class, cleanliness, social status, gender, age, perceived importance of need—none of this makes a difference to Christ.

While Jesus was relating to and restoring this unnamed woman, news comes to Jairus that his daughter has died. "When Jesus overheard what was said, he told the synagogue leader, 'Don't be afraid. Only believe'" (Mark 5:36). Imagine the roller coaster of emotions raging in Jairus. It must have taken a real act of faith to seek out Jesus and ask for the miracle. He must have been so encouraged and hopeful when Jesus agreed to come with him. Then Jairus would've been grief-stricken with the devastating news that it was too late. And then Jesus intervenes to comfort Jairus's heart: "Don't be afraid. Only believe." With those five words Jesus gives Jairus courage again, and they continue on their way to the little girl.

I love the vernacular Eugene Peterson uses in *The Message* to describe what happens next:

> They entered the leader's house and pushed their way through the gossips looking for a story and neighbors bringing in casseroles. Jesus was abrupt: "Why all this busybody grief and gossip? This child isn't dead; she's sleeping." Provoked to sarcasm, they told him he didn't know what he was talking about.
>
> But when he had sent them all out, he took the child's father and mother, along with his companions, and entered the child's room. He clasped the girl's hand and said, "*Talitha koum*," which means, "Little girl, get up." At that, she was up and walking around! This girl was twelve years of age. They, of course, were all beside themselves with joy. He gave them strict orders that no one was to know what had taken place in that room. Then he said, "Give her something to eat." (Mark 5:37–43 MSG)

At Jairus's house, Jesus sorts out the crowd. He straight up puts out everyone who isn't there for the miracle. He doesn't entertain their doubts for one second. He has a divine hatred for death and will not be delayed in conquering it:

> They do not have the faith of the woman and would undermine the faith of the father. Jesus' announcement that the girl is not dead but only sleeping meets with laughter and jeering. They are not crazy; they know when someone has died. Of course she is dead. Jesus, however, can transform a deadly storm into a great calm, a ferocious brute into a calm and gentle man, death into a calm sleep, and the laughter of scorn into the laughter of joy. Their skepticism puts them outside. There will be no miracles for the scornful throng.[4]

Jesus revives the girl and takes care of her most basic need, telling her family, "Get her something to eat." He is not content just to perform the miracle and be done, He wants to see her flourish.

LAZARUS, COME OUT

The story of Jesus raising Lazarus from the dead is fairly well-known. Jesus has learned that His close friend is at death's door, but delays and does not get to the home of Lazarus, Mary, and Martha in Bethany before Lazarus has died and already been entombed for four days. His delay in coming mystifies Lazarus's sisters. They know that Jesus loves them, and they believe that Jesus could have healed their brother if He had not postponed His arrival. They don't understand the Lord's timing. Jesus says to Lazarus's sister Martha, "Didn't I tell you that if you believed you would see the glory of God?" (John 11:40). Then the whole community gets to see the glory of God (and so do we, through the narrative in John 11). Jesus prays, then shouts, "Lazarus, come out!" (v. 43). When the dead man appears, walking out still bound in funeral linens, Jesus tells the crowd of mourners, "Unwrap him and let him go" (v. 44).

Jesus isn't rushed to perform the miracle. He wholly trusts the power of God to raise people from the dead.

There are some similarities in this story about Lazarus to the other resurrections we've been considering. Just as the little girl dies while Jesus is delayed in getting to the home of Jairus, there is a delay—an intentional one, this time—in Jesus getting to the place where the dead person is found. Jesus isn't rushed to perform the miracle. He isn't worried that if He takes a minute the miracle will be too difficult to perform. He wholly trusts the power of God to raise people from the dead. Eventually He would wait three days for His own resurrection.

In both the miracle of Jairus's daughter and the miracle of Lazarus, Jesus was sent for by loved ones. Both times, when the delay seems to be too much to overcome, He tells these loved ones to believe. He calls on Jairus, Mary, and Martha to double down on their faith in His love and power, even when their hope seems futile. He is asking them to hang on to their faith, even if it makes them look ridiculous. Will they believe in His power of life over death?

Remember how that word *compassion* contained an element of righteous indignation? The anger/compassion we have seen Jesus express in other stories is also found in the events surrounding the death of Lazarus. See especially John 11:33: "When Jesus saw her [Mary] crying, and the Jews who had come with her crying, he was deeply moved in his spirit and troubled." Jesus is troubled that things are not the way they should be. He hates the destruction and pain death brings, and He will not see it bring His dear ones heartache. Jesus' re-action to being deeply moved is that He cries: "Jesus' tears should be connected to the anger he is feeling so deeply. The public chaos surrounding him, the loud wailing and crying, and the scene of a cemetery and its reminders of death—all the result of sin and death—together produce outrage in the Son of God as he works to reverse such damage."[5]

> Just as in the beginning God used only His words to create life out of nothing, Jesus uses His words to overpower death and re-create life.

Jesus displays His authority over death itself as He commands Lazarus to get up and come out of the tomb. He spoke with similar definite authority to each of the people He would raise: "Young man, get up. Little girl, get up. Lazarus, come out." Just as in the beginning God used only His words to create life out of nothing, Jesus uses His words to overpower death and re-create life.

Jesus has dominion over death—and His own death and res-urrection was the ultimate conquering of the consequences of death, in order to give eternal life to everyone who will believe in the Savior.

Not everyone who died in ancient Palestine during the years of Jesus' ministry was raised to life again by Jesus. Though Jesus does indeed have dominion over death, we have to remember that those He raised to life again temporarily did pass away from this earth. But God had provided a way to eternal togetherness with Himself. Jesus was ushering in His kingdom. These truths can be encouraging when we're suffering or ones we love are suf-fering life-threatening disease or trauma:

> One must also be sensitive to the reality that no matter how genuine or desperate the faith, all are not healed or

saved from death. One must look beyond the moment of suffering to the eternal significance of Jesus' power. That power is related to the kingdom of God, which is present, but which is yet to be fully manifest. In the meantime, we will suffer from maladies and death. Our faith is in God's power to conquer death, not simply to restore things as they were. We can face the tragedies of everyday existence with confident faith that God is not through with us.[6]

Are you facing death? Know that Jesus is awaiting your return home. The promise is there: "The LORD cares deeply when his loved ones die" (Ps. 116:15 NLT). Jesus has gone through death for you. He did it perfectly so you could know without a shadow of a doubt that you are loved, accepted, and forgiven by God. He understands the pain that you feel. He sympathizes with you right now.

If you are grieving the death of a loved one, remember that Jesus was "deeply moved" at death too. He hates that we know this unique and seemingly unending heartache. God Himself will one day wipe away your tears, and all the saints that have gone before you will arise together and worship the God of resurrection.

thirteen

JESUS WITH THE OUTCAST

Jesus comes for sinners, for those as outcast as tax collectors and for those caught up in squalid choices and failed dreams.
BRENNAN MANNING

"Who needs a doctor: the healthy or the sick? I'm here inviting outsiders, not insiders—an invitation to a changed life, changed inside and out."
LUKE 5:31 MSG

Currently we don't have official laws that render people "outcast from society." But we certainly have people we consider "outcasts," and we don't have any trouble calling them that to the whole world via social media. Make a mistake or do something willfully wrong, and you might just be "canceled." Nothing you say matters, what you think doesn't matter—essentially, you don't matter. This is the definition of an outcast: you're outside the group and no one wants you around anymore. So, while there are no official laws casting people out, there are social ones everywhere we turn. If we are honest, we know we even create these social laws as we decide who is in and who is out on our own terms.

Most of us know what it feels like to be rejected or to be left out. Many more people feel themselves especially isolated—whether insecurities and fears keep them from better social interaction or whether the cruelty and judgment of others shuts them out.

Jesus had a special place in His heart for those who were pushed to the edge of community. The gospel narratives show us His love for the outcast, especially in the story of His encounter with the Samaritan woman at the well. The story begins,

> He had to travel through Samaria; so he came to a town of Samaria called Sychar near the property that Jacob had given his son Joseph. Jacob's well was there, and Jesus, worn out from his journey, sat down at the well. It was about noon.
>
> A woman of Samaria came to draw water.
>
> "Give me a drink," Jesus said to her, because his disciples had gone into town to buy food. (John 4:4–8)

To us, this exchange may seem ordinary, but what's actually happened here was monumental and pushed the boundaries of political correctness at the time. First, take a minute to consider how much this story shows us the humanity of Christ. Jesus is tired and needs a rest—here during the heat of the day, around noon. Even though He and His disciples are making their way to Galilee, He wisely gives Himself the needed break. Have you ever been too determined or too proud to rest, saying, "I don't need to stop! I am fine!"? Then you push through until you have a mental breakdown or blow up on someone else. We so hate to admit any weakness or need. Meanwhile, Jesus (who was God Himself) essentially said to the disciples, "Yeah, I need to stop and rest. You guys go get some food without Me."

Jesus' time-out opened the opportunity to encounter the woman who shows up at the well. It wasn't the usual time of day for women to draw their water. Most would have gone out in the morning when the day was cooler. They'd have gone together, when they were safer in a group and could hang out for a morning chat. But this Samaritan woman strategically went to the well at noon. It was shame that motivated her avoidance of the other women. She was an outsider.

Perhaps this woman felt dismay or even alarm at seeing Jesus at the well. She would immediately have recognized him as a Jew— and Jews and Samaritans did not get along. In fact, with a long history of disagreement over religious practices, Jews and Samaritans hated each other. Each one thought they were better than the other. There was real, deeply rooted racism between these two groups. The woman probably braced herself for unkind or condescending behavior from the Jew. She was more than used to this sort of treatment, but being used to it didn't lessen the pain.

CONVERSATION

So it would have surprised this woman when Jesus begins talking to her: "Give me a drink." Now to us this might sound harsh. If I was at a well to get my water for the day and some guy came up to me with this command, my knee-jerk response might be, "Get your own drink!"

But what Jesus is doing here is revolutionary! First, He is a man talking to a woman. Culturally, this was mind-blowing. Men didn't bother to talk with women they didn't know, because women were considered inferior. Jewish men believed it was inappropriate to talk to women they were not related to. This would have been scandalous. Second, Jesus was a Jew talking to a Samaritan. The racism ingrained in both ethnicities against the other should have prevented this conversation. What might sound like an abrupt command to us ("Give me a drink") was, on the contrary, a gesture of outreach. With one sentence Jesus lays waste to racism, sexism, and religious discrimination. His behavior declares that gender doesn't change His relationship toward a person. Ethnicity, shared or different, doesn't change His relationship toward a person. Religious beliefs aside, Jesus sees each person as human, first and foremost. Jesus is asking for a drink from her cup as well. (Those of you who are germophobes might hate this part.) He's willing to get that close to a Samaritan woman!

Jesus' approach toward her is gentle and humble. He's admitting His need (He's thirsty). He's acknowledging her humanness. Still, the Samaritan woman's defenses immediately go up: "'How is it that you, a Jew, ask for a drink from me, a Samaritan woman?' she asked him. For Jews do not associate with Samaritans" (John 4:9). Her nearly automatic response puts herself into the outcast category (Samaritan, woman) before the stranger can do it. She expects to be treated as an outsider. This is how she is used to being treated.

Oh, how wrong she was about Jesus! His purpose in conversing with her was completely motivated by loving her into new life:

> Jesus answered, "If you knew the gift of God, and who is
> saying to you, 'Give me a drink,' you would ask him, and he
> would give you living water."
> "Sir," said the woman, "you don't even have a bucket,
> and the well is deep. So where do you get this 'living water'?

You aren't greater than our father Jacob, are you? He gave us the well and drank from it himself, as did his sons and livestock." (John 4:10–12)

Jesus asks for a drink, but then He offers far more than a drink of water. He offers this woman Himself. Jesus points her toward salvation through relationship with God: "Everyone who drinks from this water will get thirsty again. But whoever drinks from the water that I will give him will never get thirsty again. In fact, the water I will give him will become a well of water springing up in him for eternal life" (vv. 13–14).

> While other men in her life had pursued this woman to take something from her, Jesus pursued her to give her eternal life.

The questions of the Samaritan woman don't deflect Jesus. He was on a mission. He could have taken a different way, as many Jews did, in order to avoid traveling among the hated Samaritans. But not Jesus. He meant to be at this well at this moment. Jesus and the woman at the well had a divine appointment set from eternity past in order to have this conversation. While other men in her life had pursued this woman to take something from her, Jesus pursued her to give her eternal life.

The woman responds. "'Sir,' the woman said to him, 'give me this water so that I won't get thirsty and come here to draw water'" (v. 15). Basically, she doesn't understand that Jesus is speaking in spiritual terms, so her response refers to natural thirst. Basically, "Yeah, cool. Give me the water You are talking about. I'd love not to have to come back here or be thirsty again."

Jesus knows the woman doesn't understand Him, so He takes the conversation up a notch:

"Go call your husband," he told her, "and come back here."

"I don't have a husband," she answered.

"You have correctly said, 'I don't have a husband,'" Jesus said. "For you've had five husbands, and the man you now have is not your husband. What you have said is true." (John 4:16–18)

Jesus certainly had the capacity to astonish people into giving Him their full attention. To our modern-day ears, this may sound as if Jesus is calling her on the carpet for her years of bad behavior. In truth, it's much more likely that He's reaching out to her in compassion, hoping to rescue her and give her hope in a bad situation. It's probable that this woman had been handed from man to man, with the men using her and then divorcing her. This wasn't divorce as we understand it now—with both sides being provided for with alimony and retaining social status. This woman would have had no recourse except to find another man to marry her. She'd probably had consecutive marriages in order to provide for herself financially. There would have been more severe repercussions if she'd committed adultery (the law calls for death), so we can assume that list of husbands came about through deaths or from men just being done with her. Whatever reasons for the multiple marriages, eventually she'd been unable to find a partner to take care of her.

The man she was "with" now wouldn't even marry her. No man would offer her unselfish love and commitment.

He is bringing the kingdom of God, and He invites her in. He is changing everything.

Whether this comment was laced with sarcasm, or if she was making a genuine confession by saying Jesus was a prophet, the woman immediately tries to change the subject: "'Sir,' the woman replied, 'I see that you are a prophet. Our ancestors worshiped on this mountain, but you Jews say that the place to worship is in Jerusalem'" (vv. 19–20). For sure, it must've felt like a good idea to deflect this conversation from her personal life and go back to talking about the difference between Jews and Samaritans. Deflecting helped her hide—staying out of the public eye, as she usually did.

Jesus tenderly engages her on the subject but offers her more:

> Jesus told her, "Believe me, woman, an hour is coming when you will worship the Father neither on this mountain nor in Jerusalem. You Samaritans worship what you do not know. We worship what we do know, because salvation is from the Jews. But an hour is coming, and is now here, when the true worshipers will worship the Father in Spirit and in truth. Yes, the Father wants such people to worship him. God is spirit, and those who worship him must worship in Spirit and in truth." (John 4:21–24)

Jesus wants this woman to go deeper than the subject of Jewish and Samaritan worship practices. He wants to make her think about worshiping God herself. He is bringing the kingdom of God, and He invites her in. He tells her that everyone is free to worship wherever, because He is changing everything. The place we worship doesn't matter anymore. It is *who* we worship that matters and how we can enter into true worship.

Then the woman says, perhaps with trepidation, as if she is hoping against all the odds that the Man she is talking

Whatever this woman knew about the promised Messiah, she had probably never let herself hope; her life experiences had conditioned her to believe that hope would always disappoint her.

to in the heat of the sun at midday in Samaria is actually the Messiah, "'I know that the Messiah is coming' (who is called Christ). 'When he comes, he will explain everything to us'" (v. 25). The Messiah, the "promised one," will make everything right.

The woman at the well may not have known much more about the promised Messiah, since Samaritans typically studied only the first five books of the Old Testament as their Scriptures. She may not have known that the Messiah would bear her sins and suffer in her place. She might have picked up whispers of prophesies about the Messiah based on other Scriptures, such as, "A bruised reed he will not break, and a smoldering wick he will not snuff out. In faithfulness he will bring forth justice; he will not falter or be discouraged till he establishes justice on earth. In his teaching the islands will put their hope" (Isa. 42:3–4 NIV). Or she might have heard the psalm that includes these words, "The LORD is near the brokenhearted; he saves those crushed in spirit" (Ps. 34:18). Had she heard that the Messiah would understand the feelings of an outcast because, as Psalm 22 indicates, He would be forsaken by God?

> He chooses this Samaritan woman—despised, rejected, shamed, unseen, an outcast. He lets her in on the best news, the biggest secret in the entirety of history: He is the One who will save her from her sins.

Whatever this woman knew about the promised Messiah, she had probably never let herself hope; her life experiences had conditioned her to believe that hope would always disappoint her. With each marriage she had probably hoped that this man would be the one to take care of her, to treat her like a human, and to honor her and love her instead of using her. She probably couldn't let herself actually believe that the Man at the well really was the Messiah, but her words carry the ache of longing.

And Jesus tells her, "I, the one speaking to you, am he" (v. 26).

This is the very first time Jesus reveals to someone who He really is. This hope does not put her to shame, because God's love has been poured out into her heart through the Holy Spirit, who has been given to her (see Rom. 5:5). He chooses this Samaritan woman—despised, rejected, shamed, unseen, an outcast. He lets her in on the best news, the biggest secret in the entirety of history: He is the One who will save her from her sins.

CONVERSION

The Samaritan woman has had a big gulp of that living water offered her by Jesus, and that living water is welling up inside of her just like He said it would.

> Just then his disciples arrived, and they were amazed that he was talking with a woman. Yet no one said, "What do you want?" or "Why are you talking with her?"
>
> Then the woman left her water jar, went into town, and told the people, "Come, see a man who told me everything I ever did. Could this be the Messiah?" They left the town and made their way to him. (John 4:28–30)

Without even stopping to take her water jar with her, this dear woman runs straight to meet up with all the people she's been trying to avoid. She is in such a hurry that she takes off without doing what she came to the well to do. She'd been carrying a load of shame for a long time—and she was probably still carrying it with her as she ran to tell her neighbors that Jesus was the Messiah. She tells them, "He told me everything I ever did." Her testimony is that "this man *saw* me." She is so convincing that she gets the town to come out to the well to find Jesus. She can't help herself; she has to share her good news. It's just normal to talk about what we love. The disciples, who'd gone off to the town to get food, didn't bring anybody back with them to introduce them to Jesus. But the Samaritan woman does. This scorned, shamed, unmarried, presumably childless woman has turned into an amazing evangelist.

Jesus gives value to the type of woman the church so often ignores or belittles. Jesus invited the Samaritan woman into relationship with the Messiah. He said, "Come take a drink. Come worship in spirit and in truth. Come be fully human as I am fully human. I see you, all of you, the parts you hide, the parts you are ashamed of, the parts that hurt too much to acknowledge. I see them. I will heal you. I am the one you are looking for."

> Reveal to Jesus the parts of you that are broken or that make you feel ashamed. Let Him tell you He already knows, and then enter into relationship with Him.

Are you hiding or cast out from others? Jesus has the same message for you today. Meet Him at your well, wherever that may be. Reveal to Him the parts of you that are broken or that make you feel ashamed. Let Him tell you He already knows, and then enter into relationship with Him. Then go and tell others, treating them with the same kindness and love you have received. Drink your fill of this living water and share it with others.

fourteen

JESUS WITH THE
RULE FOLLOWERS

It is easy to become distracted from Christ as the only hope for sinners. . . .
If we are good people who have lost the way but with the proper instructions
and motivation can become a better person, we need only a life coach,
not a redeemer.

MICHAEL HORTON

Looking at him, Jesus loved him and said to him, "You lack one thing: Go,
sell all you have and give to the poor, and you will have treasure in heaven.
Then come, follow me."

MARK 10:21

R ules are a good and necessary part of community living. We
need rules to help us get along together in society. But the

rules were never meant to be an end in themselves. It's no good at all when the rules of living take our eyes off the Giver of life itself.

For sure, following God's laws for us is good! The common problem is that those of us who do end up following the rules end up also taking pride in that fact. Rule followers tend to rely on the rules to make them feel righteous or right with God instead of relying on the finished work of Jesus Christ.

This parable that Jesus told explains His interactions with rule followers:

> He told his next story to some who were complacently pleased with themselves over their moral performance and looked down their noses at the common people: "Two men went up to the Temple to pray, one a Pharisee, the other a tax man. The Pharisee posed and prayed like this: 'Oh, God, I thank you that I am not like other people— robbers, crooks, adulterers, or, heaven forbid, like this tax man. I fast twice a week and tithe on all my income.'
>
> Meanwhile the tax man, slumped in the shadows, his face in his hands, not daring to look up, said, 'God, give mercy. Forgive me, a sinner.'"
>
> Jesus commented, "This tax man, not the other, went home made right with God. If you walk around with your nose in the air, you're going to end up flat on your face, but if you're content to be simply yourself, you will become more than yourself." (Luke 18:9–14 MSG)

In this case, following the rules distracted the Pharisee from truly relying on the mercy of God. Meanwhile, the tax collector who cried out, "God, give mercy. Forgive me, a sinner." was the one who went home justified. His justification came from God, not from his own works.

RICH YOUNG RULER

This idea of needing to be a follower of Christ instead of a follower of rules is clearly demonstrated in the story of the rich young ruler from Mark 10:

> As Jesus was starting out on his way to Jerusalem, a man came running up to him, knelt down, and asked, "Good Teacher, what must I do to inherit eternal life?"
>
> "Why do you call me good?" Jesus asked. "Only God is truly good. But to answer your question, you know the commandments: 'You must not murder. You must not commit adultery. You must not steal. You must not testify falsely. You must not cheat anyone. Honor your father and mother.'"
>
> "Teacher," the man replied, "I've obeyed all these commandments since I was young."
>
> Looking at the man, Jesus felt genuine love for him. "There is still one thing you haven't done," he told him. "Go and sell all your possessions and give the money to the poor, and you will have treasure in heaven. Then come, follow me."
>
> At this the man's face fell, and he went away sad, for he had many possessions. (Mark 10:17–22 NLT)

I've noticed that a common temptation for people who are rich or successful in worldly terms tends to be self-confidence—sometimes overly confident in their assumption that their own street smarts and talent got them to where they are. This rich young ruler seems to come confidently to Jesus, calling Him "Good Teacher." Jesus' answer that "Only God is truly good" seems to catch the young man off-balance. Scholars agree that Jesus offers this bit of truth about God's character to force the young man to look at who

> He was asking the man to see that true goodness—real, deep goodness—is something only God Himself could accomplish. Jesus embodied this real goodness.

God was and then in turn see who Jesus really was. Jesus *is* a Good Teacher—good in the same way that God is truly good. Jesus was trying to move this man's focus toward the only One who could save him:

This brusque response gets to the core issue raised by this encounter. The man's salutation assumes that one can find goodness in human resources and accomplishments. Probably, he identifies himself as "good" as well and asks his question from one good man to another. He wants to know how to ensure that his goodness will pay off in eternal life. He hopes that Jesus can relieve any lingering doubts about his chances and inform him if there is anything in the fine print he needs to worry about. As the scene develops, God's demands turn out to be far more costly than he bargained for, and Jesus' teaching reveals another paradox: Goodness and salvation do not come from our own valiant efforts but only as a gift from God.[1]

Jesus was asking the man to consider what the word *good* really means. He wasn't denying that He was God by saying that only God is good; instead, He was asking the man to see that true goodness—real, deep goodness—is something only God Himself could accomplish. Jesus possessed this true goodness. Jesus embodied this real goodness.

WHAT MUST I DO?

Jesus answers the rich young ruler's question, "What must I do to inherit eternal life?" by taking him first to the law and then to the gospel. The young man legitimately asked, "What must I do?" He really did think there was something he could accomplish. Jesus answers him in a very expected and seemingly welcome way. He tells him to follow the fifth, sixth, seventh, eighth, and ninth commandments. Interestingly, each of the commands that Jesus tells him to follow are all ones that are done externally, the behaviors we exercise toward other humans. The young man feels great about this response. He immediately says, "I've obeyed all these commandments since I was young." This man knew the law. He knew the commandments, and since his youth he had determined to follow those commandments. His heart must have leapt at Jesus' words. He was probably thinking, "Well, look at me! I did it!" He was like the men we read about at the opening of this chapter, "complacently pleased with themselves over their moral performance." What came next must have been a real blow to his ego, because Jesus is going to respond to this man's self-perceived goodness.

LOOKED AND LOVED

How does Jesus respond to this self-assured man? "Jesus looked at him and loved him" (Mark 10:21 NIV). He loves him. He looks at him. He sees that this man thinks he has got it all together, and Jesus feels compassion for him. Mark, as a gospel writer, doesn't throw around this word "love" lightly. This is the only time that Mark recorded that Jesus loved someone. Richard Lenski writes,

> Mark uses the higher word for "love," namely ἀγαπᾶν, the love that comprehends all that is involved and has the high, intelligent purpose to help the man in his deplorable condition; the idea is far beyond φιλεῖν, the mere love of affection, "to like." All that Jesus now tells this man is an expression of this high love for him. In every word we see

the complete comprehension of his case and the perfect purpose to help him.[2]

Jesus loved this man because this man needed Jesus' love. Jesus didn't love him because he had followed all the rules, or at least, thought he had followed all the rules. Jesus' heart was moved toward him.

Love and grace are not my own first instinctive response when I come up against people who think they are doing everything right when I in fact know they are not. If someone told me that they obeyed all the commands of God, I would exercise the hardest of eye rolls. Ironically, I would not have any reason to be so self-righteous, because I already know I don't follow these rules perfectly. Jesus, on the other hand, could have laughed in this man's face. Jesus did perfectly follow all of God's commandments, and He obeyed them beyond the letter of the law. The very heart of the commandments is a description of Jesus' heart.

Because Jesus loves this man, He decides to challenge his self-perception: "'One thing you lack,' he said. 'Go, sell everything you have and give to the poor, and you will have treasure in heaven. Then come, follow me.' At this the man's face fell. He went away sad, because he had great wealth" (Mark 10:21–22 NIV). Jesus leads this man to the end of himself. For at the very end of all his good works, Jesus is there waiting for him. Jesus tells him to sell everything and follow Him. This just breaks the man's heart. The text tells us the man had great possessions. He loved his wealth more than he loved Jesus. He wanted to follow his wealth more than he wanted to follow Jesus.

> This man finds out his goodness is not good enough. He needs the goodness of Christ.

This is the only time that the book of Mark includes someone declining an invitation to follow Jesus. This man who seemed to have it all together—who had disciplined himself to obey the commandments—couldn't give up his wealth to follow Christ. This man finds out his goodness is not good enough. He needs the goodness of another. He needs the goodness of Christ placed over his life in order to gain eternal life. What this man needs is a complete change, and not just outward compliance to a set of rules. The realization is devastating. He goes away sad. His wealth and his "goodness" mean more to him than eternal life.

Our natural tendency is to think what we do on the outside is what matters. "If I can just be a kind, honest person, all will be well." But while it is important to follow God's laws for us, His laws are not what save us. His Son saves us.

A few chapters earlier, Mark includes a conversation with a group of Pharisees that foreshadows this conversation with the sad, rich young ruler. Mark 7 shows Jesus talking with the religious leaders about what makes a person clean or unclean. They are angry at Jesus because they see the disciples eating with unwashed hands, breaking one of their many rules. Jesus then takes them to school concerning what really matters. It is a lot easier to just make sure to wash your hands before you eat than it is to admit that there is nothing you can do to make your soul good and clean. We love to rely on ourselves. We hate to admit we need something other than what we have in ourselves. We hate to admit weakness or need.

Jesus basically says to the Pharisees, or the rule keepers, "Nothing that goes into a person from outside can defile him but the things that come out of a person are what defile him" (my paraphrase). We have a deeper problem than hands not being washed before we eat. We have a deeper problem than the fact that we don't follow rules. Our problem is that our very heart is unclean, and we need someone to cleanse us from all our unrighteousness.

If sin is something I can control with my outward actions, why would I ever need a Savior? Alan Cole elaborates: "Jesus taught that sin was like a cancer, growing within us, Jew and non-Jew alike. That is far harder to deal with, for we cannot avoid it by avoiding 'infection' from others; it needs radical spiritual surgery that will change our inner nature."[3]

He calls you to give up on your self-salvation project and to come to the end of your rope, where He is waiting for you.

If you feel you have kept all the rules, if you have relied solely on yourself for saving, or if you think your own goodness is the most important thing, know that Jesus sees you and loves you. You must be tired, angry, and sad. He calls you to give up on your self-salvation project and to come to the end of your rope, where He is waiting for you. He calls you to give up on your own goodness being good enough, and to trust in His goodness toward you and for you.

Martin Luther famously said, "God doesn't need your good work, but your neighbor does."[4] This is why Jesus called on the rich young man to give up all he had and give it to the poor. When you are loving others from a heart of love instead of "doing the right thing so God will love you," your love will be radically generous and radically free. When we give out of love instead of trying to earn the right to call ourselves good or to have God be pleased with us, that love will be grace-filled. When we don't think we have to earn love, we won't make others do it either. There is such a deep freedom awaiting you.

Give up all you have. Give up all you trust in. Follow Him.

fifteen

JESUS WITH THOSE WHO HATED HIM

Love has within it a redemptive power. And there is a power there that eventually transforms individuals. . . . This is why Jesus says love. There's something about love that builds up and is creative. There is something about hate that tears down and is destructive. So love your enemies.

MARTIN LUTHER KING JR.

"Love your enemies and pray for those who persecute you."

MATTHEW 5:44

Y ou're probably noticing by now how much Jesus loved—and how much He was loved in return by a great many people. His love created love in multitudes of people. But I would be remiss if I neglected to mention how much people hated Jesus as well. The religious elite of the day were the ones who led the charge in despising and maligning Jesus. As we read the Bible, we like to distance ourselves from these religious elite. We like to think of ourselves as the ones who would have loved and followed Jesus. But it's a good practice to take a minute to examine our own hearts and attitudes and question who we would have aligned with if we were walking in the same cities as Jesus.

WHO WERE THE PHARISEES?

You might be tempted to skim this section thinking you may already know who the Pharisees were. But let me stretch your understanding. The Pharisees were not a hated group among the Jewish people. They were fine, upstanding citizens who were involved in the community. No one questioned their morals or their devotion to Judaism or the Torah. They were a powerful force. They were well thought of. They were the ones you didn't mind being seen with. While we typically think of them as ones who followed every single rule, the truth is that they knew the law was impossible to follow. It is more accurate to think of them as a group of people who "appreciated the weaknesses of human nature and adjusted the impossibly high standards of the Law so as to take into account the realities of life."[1] This explains why they hated Jesus so much. They wanted to make the commands of God achievable, but Jesus wouldn't have that. Jesus wouldn't allow them to think that. Jesus was the only One who was able to perfectly fulfill the law. He wouldn't let the religious leadership

The gospel is a hard word for people who think they have their lives together. Jesus was upfront about the fact that the law wouldn't save them; only He could.

dumb down the perfect commands of God: "The Pharisaic regulations were numerous and aggravating, but at least they could be fulfilled. . . . And a muted sense of one's sin goes hand in hand with a false sense of spiritual security; the need to depend on God's mercy no longer appears crucial."[2]

Jesus did this so that they wouldn't be able to rely on themselves or their interpretation of the law. He did this so that they would see how desperately they needed something, or more specifically Someone, outside of themselves in order to be accepted by God. They wanted a righteousness or a right standing before God based on their own works. This is why the gospel is a hard word for people who think they have their lives together. Jesus was upfront with them about the fact that the law wouldn't save them; only He could. This is why they hated Jesus.

As you read multiple conversations Jesus carries on with these religious leaders, you can see why He aggravated them. He didn't pull His punches, so to speak. He was a truth-teller. John 10:24–30 records one of these plain-speaking conversations:

> The Jews who were there gathered around him, saying, "How long will you keep us in suspense? If you are the Messiah, tell us plainly."
>
> Jesus answered, "I did tell you, but you do not believe. The works I do in my Father's name testify about me, but you do not believe because you are not my sheep. My sheep listen to my voice; I know them, and they follow me. I give them eternal life, and they shall never perish; no one will snatch them out of my hand. My Father, who has given them to me, is greater than all; no one can snatch them out of my Father's hand. I and the Father are one." (NIV)

When they ask outright if Jesus is the Messiah, Jesus doesn't shy away from the conversation. He responds that He has already told them, and has done miracles to confirm what He told them—and still they don't believe. But then He really offends them by saying the reason they don't believe is that they aren't the Father's. Yikes! If the Jews claimed anything it was that they particularly were children of God. This was a slap in the face. But Jesus was not just arbitrarily trying to offend the Jews. He was trying to give them the truth so they could experience eternal life and eternal security. The Pharisees wanted none of it. They figured they were saved by right of their birth as Jews. They rested on their ethnicity instead of repenting and resting in their Savior. They believed in their identity instead of the claims of Jesus. This call to give up all that they had wrongly placed their hope in only infuriated them further. But Jesus still calls to them. He must offend them to save them.

ROCKED

Speaking the truth can get you in a lot of trouble. These irate Jewish leaders want Jesus dead: "Again the Jews picked up rocks to stone him" (John 10:31). There are only two possible responses when you've been told you can't save yourself: you either believe and receive, or you reject the message and give yourself over to anger.

This isn't the first time the Pharisees have wanted to kill Jesus, and it won't be the last either. But it isn't the right time for His death. Jesus says to them, "I have shown you many good works from the Father. For which of these works are you stoning me?" (v. 32). He presses them to think past their rage to question themselves. Why do they hate him? He reminds them of the good things He has done—healing the sick, feeding those in need, raising the dead, releasing those possessed by demons. These are all life-giving acts. He asks them, in effect, "Which one of these things is worthy of your hatred and worthy of My death?"

"'We aren't stoning you for a good work,' the Jews answered, 'but for blasphemy, because you—being a man—make yourself God'" (v. 33). They hate His truth claim. They hate that He is demanding their allegiance. They hate that He is telling them that their "religiosity" means nothing and that they need Him. They understand what He is claiming, and this is what makes them despise Him.

Jesus meets these hard-hearted leaders with truth. He engages with them. He gives them the saving message of faith in the Messiah.

Jesus wielded truth like a cudgel against the wall of unbelief:

> We see that the preceding events happened in the synagogue. Instead of taking to heart what Jesus said, dropping their presumptions, and allowing themselves to be humbled so that God might thus bless them through Jesus they went into a rage at what they heard. Many modern preachers would regard this as the gravest kind of mistake on Jesus' part. They think it the part of wisdom to be soft and yielding toward unbelief and presumption and never to strike it down with the cudgel of the law. But Jesus kept causing commotions like this, and Peter and James followed his example (Acts 4:10, 19, 20), so did all the apostles (Acts 5:30–32), likewise Stephen (Acts 7:51–54). The harder the unbelief, the harder the blows it receives from Jesus.[3]

Jesus meets hardness of heart with the hard truth. And yet He still meets these hard-hearted leaders with truth. He doesn't ignore their questions. He engages with them. He gives them the saving message of faith in the Messiah.

I AM THE SON OF GOD

Jesus tries one more time. He makes another attempt to get these people to believe instead of deny:

> Jesus answered them, "Isn't it written in your law, I said, you are gods? If he called those to whom the word of God came 'gods'—and the Scripture cannot be broken—do you say, 'You are blaspheming' to the one the Father set apart and sent into the world, because I said: I am the Son of God? If I am not doing my Father's works, don't believe me. But if I am doing them and you don't believe me, believe the works. This way you will know and understand that the Father is in me and I in the Father." (John 10:34–38)

Jesus is pleading now. "If you don't believe My words, believe all the works that I have done. You can't deny what you have seen with your own eyes." And yet they do. These leaders ignore what He has done. They ignore His goodness. They stop their ears to His call home.

With that, the matter is settled: "Then they were trying again to seize him, but he escaped their grasp" (v. 39). These men are even angrier now than they were when they were shouting about stoning Jesus! Remember who Jesus is: He and the Father are one. All power belongs to Him. He could have with a single word destroyed these people. And yet how does He respond? "He escaped their grasp." The narrative doesn't explain how Jesus got away. I like to imagine there's some sort of Jedi mind trick ("These aren't the droids you are looking for"), and then He is gone, off to find a group of people who will believe His claims. Richard Lenski offers this suggestion:

Did Jesus use his miraculous power to pass from the brow of the hill through the midst of the murderous mob? Many deny it and think it enough to refer to the majesty of Jesus' person but forget that this majesty did not deter this mob from bringing Jesus to this precipice to kill him. And right here, when one thrust would have done it, Jesus walks calmly through the crowd and, altogether unmolested, walks on his way and leaves Nazareth forever. This sign of his miraculous might Jesus left them in order to strike dismay into their hearts, to lead them to repentance, if possible, to warn them of his power of judgment if they continued obdurate.[4]

Jesus doesn't destroy this angry mob. He wishes them to come to repentance, so He gives them more time. He never stops telling these hard-hearted ones, even during His trial and death, who He was and what He came to do. He wanted to save His people from their sins. He loved His enemies.

For those of you who are unsure about Jesus and His truth claims, for those of you who aren't even sure why you are reading this book because you hate what Jesus claims, for those of you who have loved ones who hate Jesus, remember that Jesus continues to call. He continues to invite. He desires for you to believe. He is patient. He will give you the truth over and over and over. Please hear, trust, and believe.

sixteen

JESUS WITH
HIS BETRAYER

*Why shouldn't I hate her? She did the worst thing to me that anyone can
do to anyone else. Let them believe that they're loved and wanted and then
show them that it's all a sham.*

AGATHA CHRISTIE

But Jesus said to him, "Judas, are you betraying the Son of Man with a kiss?"

LUKE 22:48

Betrayal is an intimate act. You cannot be betrayed by those
who have no access to your life or love. Betrayal must take
place when supposed friendship or love is present. Lando Calris-
sian, Alfred Redl, Peter Pettigrew, Cypher, Marcus Junius Brutus—

these names are synonymous with betrayal. Fictitious or real, each were trusted allies, and each one did the unthinkable. Their acts of treachery came as a devastating surprise to those who had faith in them. Some had redemption arcs to their stories; others ended tragically, like Judas Iscariot. The question for us as we read about Judas's final hours with Jesus is, "How would you treat the person you knew was about to betray you?" In most stories, everything would have turned out differently had the betrayer been exposed to the betrayed ahead of time. Jesus knew Judas's terrible plan, and God's Word shows us how this perfect Man interacted with Judas.

JESUS WASHES FEET

Jesus treated Judas with love and intimate friendship, along with the other disciples.

> Before the Passover Festival, Jesus knew that his hour had come to depart from this world to the Father. Having loved his own who were in the world, he loved them to the end.
>
> Now when it was time for supper, the devil had already put it into the heart of Judas, Simon Iscariot's son, to betray him. Jesus knew that the Father had given everything into his hands, that he had come from God, and that he was going back to God. So he got up from supper, laid aside his outer clothing, took a towel, and tied it around himself. Next, he poured water into a basin and began to wash his disciples' feet and to dry them with the towel tied around him. (John 13:1–5)

This foot-washing takes place on the evening before the crucifixion. Jesus and His disciples are about to partake in the "Last Supper." Jesus knows His time has come. He knows these are His last hours with the Twelve: "Jesus knew that his hour had come to depart from this world to the Father. Having loved his own who were in the world, he loved them to the end." So, He once again talks with them about who He is and what He is about. He does this in a way that will symbolize what is ultimately about to happen. He lays aside his outer clothing and cleans away the dirt, the grime, the stains. He washes His disciples' feet. It is important to take notice of the fact that Jesus knew Judas was going to betray Him and yet still He lowered Himself to wash His betrayer's feet.

Their leader took on the role of a servant in order to wash His disciples' feet. This act would have rocked the disciples to their core: "Even if a guest had bathed just before attending a banquet, his feet would be dirty from dusty roads. The lowest of the slaves—in Jewish households, a Gentile slave—was made to do the menial work of bathing guests' feet."[1] Washing feet was menial. No self-respecting Jew would have done this, let alone a rabbi. This dirty work was reserved for the slaves. And yet here is our Jesus. Here is the God-Man, surprising His followers yet another time. With this intimate act of care, Jesus avows the value of each of these image bearers, even His betrayer's.

> **The God-Man surprises His followers yet another time. With this intimate act of care, Jesus avows the value of each of these image bearers, even His betrayer's.**

JESUS SHARES A MEAL

While this act of washing feet is intimate for so many reasons, Jesus doesn't stop there. He shares a meal with Judas. He continues doing what He has done for years with this man, but this night He does it knowing what will happen in the next few hours:

He was troubled in his spirit and testified, "Truly I tell you, one of you will betray me."

The disciples started looking at one another—uncertain which one he was speaking about. One of his disciples, the one Jesus loved, was reclining close beside Jesus. Simon Peter motioned to him to find out who it was he was talking about. So he leaned back against Jesus and asked him, "Lord, who is it?"

Jesus replied, "He's the one I give the piece of bread to after I have dipped it." When he had dipped the bread, he gave it to Judas, Simon Iscariot's son. After Judas ate the piece of bread, Satan entered him. So Jesus told him, "What you're doing, do quickly."

None of those reclining at the table knew why he said this to him. Since Judas kept the money-bag, some thought that Jesus was telling him, "Buy what we need for the festival," or that he should give something to the poor. After receiving the piece of bread, he immediately left. And it was night. (John 13:21–30)

Jesus washes Judas, then He feeds him. He gives Judas bread. This is "usually a sign of honor and care."[2] Jesus acknowledges that He knows what Judas is about to do and asks him to go do it quickly. What pain must have been rending His heart at that very moment. Our verses even say, "He was deeply troubled in His spirit." Jesus, a human person, felt the pain of betrayal just as you or I would. One of the Twelve, one of the original followers, would now be the one to turn and betray Him.

What made Judas do it? What turned him into a betrayer? The tipping event was another time when someone showed true affection. Only a few days earlier, when Jesus "was reclining at the table, a woman came with an alabaster jar of very expensive perfume of pure nard. She broke the jar and poured it on his head. But some were expressing indignation to one another: 'Why has this perfume been wasted? For this perfume might have been sold for more than three hundred denarii and given to the poor.' And they began to scold her" (Mark 14:3–5).

Remember this story? Judas was the one "expressing indignation" at this extravagant show of love and affection. When this woman, overwhelmed by her love for Christ, gave everything she had to show it, Judas hated it and let everyone know. Jesus' reply to Judas is the impetus for the betrayal, the straw that broke the betrayer's back: "Jesus replied, 'Leave her alone. Why are you bothering her?'" (v. 6). Jesus did have a few more words for Judas, and then we read this: "Then Judas Iscariot, one of the Twelve, went to the chief priests to betray Jesus to them. And when they heard this, they were glad and promised to give him money. So he started looking for a good opportunity to betray him" (vv. 10–11). The repentant woman's love for Jesus, and His love in return, sent Judas to the chief priests.

Even over their last dinner, Jesus knew this betrayal was coming. The only thing Jesus asks of him is to do it quickly. Just get it over with. The pain Jesus felt had to be severe. Judas obliges Christ's request and leaves the meal. He goes and does the unthinkable. He brings those who want to kill Jesus to the place where Jesus is crying out to the Father in the garden of Gethsemane: "Suddenly a mob came, and one of the Twelve named Judas was leading them. He came near Jesus to kiss him, but Jesus said to him, 'Judas, are you betraying the Son of Man with a kiss?'" (Luke 22:47–48).

Judas wasn't just in the crowd—he was leading the crowd. He comes up to Jesus, feigning to display the kind of loving intimacy Christ had truly shown him earlier. He comes with a fake show of affection, a fake show of love to the One who embodied love and affection. Judas doesn't just kiss Jesus once either: "Matthew and Mark use the compound verb which means to shower with kisses, *abkuessen*. Judas prolonged the act as if to tell the captors: 'See, this is the man you want!'"[3] Judas mimics the woman he watched kiss the feet of Christ. He kisses over and over again. He knows no real love for Christ, but he uses the means he has seen others display. He betrays the One who has no false or empty emotion in His heart. To this betrayal Jesus just asks him one question: "Friend, why have you come?" (Matt. 26:50). Jesus is still calling him *friend*. Betrayed with a kiss, friend—this is how? This false show of love is one more stab into the heart of Jesus.

JESUS HEALS

It's a heartbreaking night. When the disciples want to fight, Jesus tells them once again that this is not what He is about or what His kingdom is for. Jesus is here to help, not to hurt. He tells them, "Or do you think that I cannot call on my Father, and he will provide me here and now with more than twelve legions of angels?" (Matt. 26:53). He doesn't need their protection or aggression. He quite literally can take care of Himself, but He knew His time had come.

Jesus can quite literally take care of Himself. But from the very beginning, His ministry was about taking care of others.

He wasn't moving forward to take care of Himself. From the very beginning, His ministry was about taking care of others.

Peter slashes off the ear of one of the mob, and Jesus does what He always does: He heals and restores (Luke 22:50–51). Jesus even helps the ones who come to kill him: "Judas betrays Jesus with a kiss, and Jesus, in mercy, heals the servant's severed ear. The conflict between Jesus and the forces of darkness escalates. This darkness still would surround us. Yet, God used the night of betrayal to overcome the darkness and usher in His everlasting light."[4]

The end of Judas's story is a tragic one. He hangs himself. I can't help but wonder what would have happened if Judas had not isolated himself after he betrayed Christ. What would have happened if he had come back around to see the other disciples? Peter also failed tragically during this time but was restored. Peter was reminded that he was already forgiven, but Judas only saw his failure. I can't help but believe that Jesus would have offered forgiveness to Judas if Judas had sought Him out. We see this by the way that Jesus ends his life whispering from the cross, "Father, forgive them, because they do not know what they are doing" over the very men who were killing and mocking Him (Luke 23:34). Surely this forgiveness would have reached for Judas as well. Although we don't know what happened before Judas took his final breath, whether or not he repented of his sin, I do know my Jesus, who would have granted forgiveness if it was sought. How like God would it be to find out that Judas had made it into heaven as well? Next to me, next to you, there he kneels, the betrayer. It wouldn't surprise me one bit.

In Jesus, you can know the fullness of forgiveness, love, and acceptance.

So, if you have betrayed Christ in ways you never thought possible, if you're struggling to get past what you have done, remember that Jesus gives forgiveness. He gives intimacy, He wants you to be clean. He wants you to be fed. He gives His body broken for you. He sheds His blood for you. In Jesus, you can know the fullness of forgiveness, love, and acceptance. Believe. Receive. Rejoice.

seventeen

JESUS WITH YOU

Make your home with me. • *Come to me* • *Learn from me.* • *Get away with me.*
Follow me. • *Remain in my love.* • *I call you friends.*
Abide in me. • *Live in me.*
JESUS, IN THE GOSPELS

Maybe you have already found yourself in many pages of this book, especially if you see yourself as a doubter, a denier, or a discouraged one. Maybe you recognize that you need healing—physical or emotional or spiritual. Maybe you're a rule follower, or maybe you're a betrayer. Whether or not you fit several or none of these categories, Jesus offers you an invitation to draw near.

COME HOME

The first part of Jesus' invitation is for you to come home—come home to abide in Him.

> "Live in me. Make your home in me just as I do in you. In the same way that a branch can't bear grapes by itself but only by being joined to the vine, you can't bear fruit unless you are joined with me.
>
> "I am the Vine, you are the branches. When you're joined with me and I with you, the relation intimate and organic, the harvest is sure to be abundant. Separated, you can't produce a thing. Anyone who separates from me is deadwood, gathered up and thrown on the bonfire. But if you make yourselves at home with me and my words are at home in you, you can be sure that whatever you ask will be listened to and acted upon. This is how my Father shows who he is—when you produce grapes, when you mature as my disciples.
>
> "I've loved you the way my Father has loved me. Make yourselves at home in my love. If you keep my commands, you'll remain intimately at home in my love. That's what I've done—kept my Father's commands and made myself at home in his love.
>
> "I've told you these things for a purpose: that my joy might be your joy, and your joy wholly mature. This is my command: Love one another the way I loved you. This is the very best way to love. Put your life on the line for your friends. You are my friends when you do the things I command you. I'm no longer calling you servants because servants don't understand what their master is thinking and planning. No, I've named you friends because I've let you in on everything I've heard from the Father.

"You didn't choose me, remember; I chose you, and put you in the world to bear fruit, fruit that won't spoil. As fruit bearers, whatever you ask the Father in relation to me, he gives you.

"But remember the root command: Love one another."
(John 15:4–17 MSG)

This invitation is for you. It's your invitation to make yourself at home in the love of Jesus. We spend so much of our lives feeling out of place or not at home. Jesus is what we are looking for. His invitation is what we are craving. We bounce from distraction to distraction, trying our hardest to find inner peace, rest, and home, when all the while home is actually calling to us and opening up the way for us to find our way there. James K. A. Smith talks about this homeward journey in his book *On the Road with Saint Augustine*. He writes,

> The soul's hunger for peace is a longing for a kind of rest from anxiety and frantic pursuits—it is to rest *in* God. And for Augustine, to find this rest—to entrust ourselves to the one who holds us—is to find *joy*. "In your gift we find our rest," Augustine concludes. "There are you our joy. Our rest is our peace." Joy, for Augustine, is characterized by the quietude that is the opposite of anxiety—the exhale of someone who has been holding her breath out of fear or worry or insecurity. It is the blissful rest of someone who realizes she no longer has to perform; she is loved. We find joy in the grace of God precisely because he is the one we don't have to prove anything to. But it is also the exhale of someone who has arrived—who can finally breathe after making it through the anxiety-inducing experience of the border crossing, seeking refuge, subject to the capricious whims of

a world and system that could turn on her at any moment. What we long for is an escape not from creaturehood but from the fraught, harrowing experience of being human in a broken world. What we are hoping for is a place where a sovereign Lord can assure us, "You're safe here."[1]

When you read about a safe place to exhale, doesn't your heart long for it? Don't you desire to lay down your doubting and denying and fear and faintheartedness and just lie down to rest in the Father's house? John 15 records Jesus calling us to that very thing! Come home. Live in Christ's love for the sinners, the sufferers, the seekers, the doubters, and the discouraged. Live in His love for you. Abide in it. Get cozy there. This is what we will be doing for the rest of eternity, learning to be fully at home with the love God shows us.

The type of love we find in Christ is not a love we have ever known. His love is perfection, in the most literal sense of the word. Christ's love for us mirrors the way the Father loves the Son: "I've loved you the way my Father has loved me" (John 15:9–10). Frederick Bruner expands this idea:

> "Just as much as the Father loved me—there! that is how much I have loved you. Make your home in this special love of mine (and relax)." Jesus invites us to make ourselves at home in his love for us, which is a love that is just as large as his Father's love for him. This fact should overwhelm us—to the point that we can relax a bit in our new home when we think of our homemaker (and so my parenthesized addition—"and relax"—to catch the sense of Jesus' remarkable promise). Out of this huge well of divine love we can draw the love we need as we move out with our much tinier containers into a love-starved world. We do not have

the resources of love we need within ourselves; but in our living room with Jesus, "at home" with him and his family, we have a well of love—from the Father through the Son by the Spirit and for us (!)—and so we can constantly draw from this deep well into our pitiable containers. *"Make your home in this special love of mine."*[2]

Jesus takes the lead and makes the home. He doesn't just passively sit by and watch you flounder in your emotions or situation. He sees your need for a home. He sees you need Him. So He provides Himself. God took this initiative with us: "For God so loved the world that he gave" (John 3:16 NIV). "We love because he first loved us" (1 John 4:19). His loving creates in us a love for Him. The desire for home is a desire to be with the One who loves us. His love generates that desire. There is one place where we can fully be ourselves, put our feet up on the couch, wear comfortable pants and a sweatshirt, not worry about whether our teeth are clean or our breath stinks. There is one place where every sin and foible are known. There is one place where we are accepted and treasured and chosen. There is one place where we don't have to fake a smile or pretend to laugh. The one place where we are known and loved is with Him, with Love. There our hearts are changed and softened. There we desire to love God back, and there our desire to love others is ignited.

The one place where we are known and loved is with Him, with Love.

God's love has provided everything for us; all we have to do is admit that we need Him, we need home, and nothing we can do can earn us a seat at the table:

> Just as Jesus is the recipient of the Father's love, so the disciples are the recipients of his love. Jesus' statement that

he "loved" his disciples employs the aorist tense, depicting his love as a complete action, denoting perhaps the entire demonstration of Jesus' love for his disciples throughout his time with them and culminating in his death for them.[3]

Jesus' life, death, and resurrection are our forever key to the home we have always wanted.

The way we love others starts by knowing we are loved.

Jesus tells the disciples that the way the world will know we are His is by the way we love each other—and that includes the others who are doubters, discouraged, fearful, fainthearted, wanderers, needy, sick, or sad. The way we love others starts by knowing we are loved. We take the other pilgrims and show them the way home, the way to Love. We listen to the voice of our Friend, and we help others hear that voice too. When others can't hear Jesus calling, we remind them that He is. We make a space for the rest of the crowd to be silenced and we help them tune their ears to hear His call.

BE FREE

Jesus doesn't just invite us home to His love. He also invites us to rest and freedom.

Jesus resumed talking to the people, but now tenderly. "The Father has given me all these things to do and say. This is a unique Father-Son operation, coming out of Father and Son intimacies and knowledge. No one knows the Son the way the Father does, nor the Father the way the Son does. But I'm not keeping it to myself; I'm ready to go over it line by line with anyone willing to listen.

"Are you tired? Worn out? Burned out on religion?

Come to me. Get away with me and you'll recover your life. I'll show you how to take a real rest. Walk with me and work with me—watch how I do it. Learn the unforced rhythms of grace. I won't lay anything heavy or ill-fitting on you. Keep company with me and you'll learn to live freely and lightly." (Matt. 11:27–30 MSG)

The home we find in Christ Jesus isn't a home where we feel the incessant need to earn our keep, but rather a place where rest and freedom motivate us to love and care for those around us because Christ has already earned our place. This true home is where we can finally admit that we are worn out and that, quite frankly, "We are over it." This true home is a place where we can be at peace within ourselves and with the way God has made us. It is a place where we can learn about grace. It is a place where we can keep company with Christ. It is freedom.

This invitation to freedom is for all those who are harassed and helpless. It is for those who are hurried and hapless. It is for every single person you see hurrying by you every single day of your life. It is for you. Believe it is for you. Jesus said, "Come to me, *all* of you who are weary and burdened" (Matt. 11:28, emphasis added). When you see someone walking in the grocery store, believe this verse is for that person too. There is not a single living soul who isn't weary and burdened. We all are. We are burned by our sin. We are weary from the ways others have sinned against us. We are all included in Christ's invitation.

We often feel like we need to earn our way into the party—or maybe that is what you were taught your entire life. Maybe you were taught to earn your way to anything good or valuable. Jesus is calling you to a place of *unearning*. He is calling you to a place of resting in what He has earned on your behalf.

Jesus refers to Himself as "gentle and humble in heart" (Matt. 11:28). He doesn't lord it over you that He has earned your keep; He asks you to rejoice in His earning. Jesus Himself says He didn't come to condemn but rather to save the world. He came for the sick. He came for the needy. He came for those who weren't pulling it off. He came for those who could barely get out of bed in the morning. His very mission was to do the work that needed to be done to make us right before the Father. "Come to me and I will *give* you rest," He said. His heart is set on giving. Just as the Father gave the Son, so the Son gives to us. He gives us His perfect record of being the One who could always obey the law of God. He gives us the forgiveness we so desperately need. He gives us life everlasting. He gives us our forever home. He is generous beyond anything we have ever known. He holds no goodness back from us.

The rest Jesus gives us is a full and complete rest. We can rest from all the things we think we have to do to make God love us more. We can rest from all the ways we try to earn favor. We can rest from all the guilt we have for all the sins we have committed. We can rest from our inner lawyer's continuous monologue demanding that we "do more and try harder." We can rest from the rehashing of all the ways we have failed. We can rest from the rehashing of all the ways that we have succeeded. We can rest from trying to grab what we already have. We have the love of the Father. We have forgiveness of sins. We have a place where we belong. We have a home. We have a family.

This rest comes from the Man who knew perfect peace. He knew perfect peace with His Father. He knew perfect peace within Himself. He always lived into the identity of the beloved Son. He knew perfect peace with others. We have seen how Jesus loved and lived. He knew perfect peace with the creation, which He subdued in order to heal and save His children.

This One of perfect peace is calling, beckoning you—yes, even you—to come home and find rest in His love. Will you do that today? Will you do that even now? Acknowledge your need. Acknowledge your Savior. Acknowledge His love. Welcome home.

The eleven disciples traveled to Galilee, to the mountain where Jesus had directed them. When they saw him, they worshiped, but some doubted. Jesus came near and said to them, "All authority has been given to me in heaven and on earth. Go, therefore, and make disciples of all nations, baptizing them in the name of the Father and of the Son and of the Holy Spirit, teaching them to observe everything I have commanded you. And remember, I am with you always, to the end of the age." (Matt. 28:16–20)

ACKNOWLEDGMENTS

Thank you to my family. As always, your support, kindness, prayers, teasing, and love have sustained me.

Thank you to my church family, RISEN; you are the ones who believe in me more than I believe in myself. Thank you for loving me and encouraging me in dark times and for laughing and dancing with me in happy times.

To the offbeat group of women in my community group, you all make me laugh and give me freedom to be exactly who I am. I love you!

There are loads of people—too many to name—who disciple me from afar. They don't even know how much they impact my life as I stalk their social media and read nearly everything they write.

NOTES

INTRODUCTION: LOVED THEM TO THE END

Epigraph: Brennan Manning, *The Ragamuffin Gospel* (Colorado Springs: Multnomah Books, 2015), 26.

CHAPTER 1: JESUS, THE MOST COMPLETE HUMAN

1. Lisa Sharon Harper, *The Very Good Gospel: How Everything Wrong Can Be Made Right* (Colorado Springs: Waterbrook Publishing, 2016), 113.

CHAPTER 2: JESUS WITH THE DOUBTERS

Epigraph: Os Guinness, *God in the Dark: The Assurance of Faith Beyond a Shadow of Doubt* (Wheaton, IL: Crossway Books, 1996), 14.

1. Michael Joseph Brown, "The Gospel of Matthew," in *True to Our Native Land: An African American New Testament Commentary*, ed. Brian K. Blount et al. (Minneapolis: Fortress Press, 2007), 102.

2. Frederick Dale Bruner, *The Gospel of John: A Commentary* (Grand Rapids, MI: Eerdmans, 2012), 815.

3. Tokunboh Adeyemo, ed., *Africa Bible Commentary* (Grand Rapids, MI: Zondervan, 2006), 1276.

CHAPTER 3: JESUS WITH THE DISCOURAGED

Epigraph: Paul E. Miller, *Love Walked Among Us: Learning to Love Like Jesus* (Colorado Springs: NavPress, 2014), 36.

1. Frederick William Danker, ed., *A Greek-English Lexicon of the New Testament and Other Early Christian Literature*, 3rd ed. (Chicago: University of Chicago Press, 2000), 933.
2. Darrell L. Bock, *The NIV Application Commentary: Luke* (Grand Rapids, MI: Zondervan, 1996), 615.
3. R. T. France, *Matthew: An Introduction and Commentary*, vol. 1, Tyndale New Testament Commentaries (Downers Grove, IL: InterVarsity Press, 1985), 179.
4. Tokunboh Adeyemo, ed., *Africa Bible Commentary* (Grand Rapids, MI: Zondervan, 2006), 1156.

CHAPTER 4: JESUS WITH THE DENIERS

Epigraph: Chad Bird, "Excuse Me, But Your Soul Is Showing," 1517 (blog), September 17, 2019, https://www.1517.org/articles/excuse-me-but-your-soul-is-showing.

1. Darrell L. Bock, *The NIV Application Commentary: Luke* (Grand Rapids, MI: Zondervan, 1996), 576.
2. Donald Guthrie, "John," in *New Bible Commentary: 21st Century Edition*, ed. D. A. Carson et al., 4th ed. (Downers Grove, IL: InterVarsity Press, 1994), 1065.

CHAPTER 5: JESUS WITH THE FAINTHEARTED

Epigraph: C. S. Lewis, *The Voyage of the Dawn Treader* (New York: HarperCollins, 1980), 187.

1. Michael J. Wilkins, *The NIV Application Commentary: Matthew* (Grand Rapids, MI: Zondervan, 2004), 516.
2. Ibid., 517.
3. Ibid.

CHAPTER 6: JESUS WITH THE FAILURE

Epigraph: Daniel Emery Price, *Scandalous Stories: A Sort of Commentary on the Parables* (Irvine, CA: 1517 Publishing, 2018), 6.

1. R. C. H. Lenski, *The Interpretation of St. Luke's Gospel* (Minneapolis: Augsburg Publishing House, 1961), 422–23.
2. C. H. Spurgeon, *Spurgeon's Sermons on New Testament Women*, vol. 1 (Grand Rapids, MI: Kregel Publications, 1994), 68.
3. Price, *Scandalous Stories*, 6.

CHAPTER 7: JESUS WITH THE FEARFUL

Epigraph: Frederick Buechner, *Beyond Words: Daily Readings in the ABC's of Faith* (New York: HarperCollins, 2004), 242.

1. Joel B. Green, *The Gospel of Luke*, The New International Commentary on the New Testament (Grand Rapids, MI: Eerdmans, 1997), 482.
2. Luke 12:4–5 MSG.
3. Green, *The Gospel of Luke*, 482.
4. R. C. H. Lenski, *The Interpretation of St. Luke's Gospel* (Minneapolis: Augsburg Publishing House, 1961), 677.

CHAPTER 8: JESUS WITH THE FORGOTTEN

Epigraph: Alia Joy, *Glorious Weakness: Discovering God in All We Lack* (Grand Rapids, MI: Baker Books, 2019), 129.

1. C. S. Lewis, *The Weight of Glory* (New York: HarperOne, 2001), 45.
2. John Nolland, *The Gospel of Matthew: A Commentary on the Greek Text*, New International Greek Testament Commentary (Grand Rapids, MI: Eerdmans, 2005), 1029–30.
3. Frederick Dale Bruner, *Matthew: A Commentary: The Churchbook, Matthew 13–28*, vol. 2 (Grand Rapids, MI: Eerdmans, 2007), 569.
4. Ibid., 569–70.
5. Ibid.

CHAPTER 9: JESUS WITH THOSE IN DANGER

1. Gary M. Burge, *The NIV Application Commentary: John* (Grand Rapids, MI: Zondervan, 2000), 245.

2. Frederick Dale Bruner, *The Gospel of John: A Commentary* (Grand Rapids, MI: Eerdmans, 2012), 505–506.
3. Ibid., 506.
4. Colin G. Kruse, *John: An Introduction and Commentary*, vol. 4, Tyndale New Testament Commentaries (Downers Grove, IL: InterVarsity Press, 2003), 200.
5. Burge, *John*, 247–48.

CHAPTER 10: JESUS WITH THOSE WHO NEED HEALING

1. St. Augustine, quoted in Anders Nygren, *Agape and Eros* (London: SPCK, 1957), 536.
2. David E. Garland, *The NIV Application Commentary: Mark* (Grand Rapids, MI: Zondervan, 1996), 203.
3. Ibid.
4. Ibid.
5. R. T. France, *The Gospel of Mark*, New International Greek Testament Commentary (Grand Rapids, MI: Eerdmans, 2002), 117–18.
6. R. Alan Cole, *Mark: An Introduction and Commentary*, vol. 2, Tyndale New Testament Commentaries (Downers Grove, IL: InterVarsity Press, 1989), 118–19.
7. Garland, *Mark*, 82.

CHAPTER 11: JESUS WITH THOSE IN NEED

1. Gary M. Burge, *The NIV Application Commentary: John* (Grand Rapids, MI: Zondervan, 2000), 91.
2. R. Alan Cole, *Mark: An Introduction and Commentary*, vol. 2, Tyndale New Testament Commentaries (Downers Grove, IL: InterVarsity Press, 1989), 196–97.
3. James R. Edwards, *The Gospel According to Mark*, The Pillar New Testament Commentary (Grand Rapids, MI: Eerdmans, 2002), 232.
4. Frederick Dale Bruner, The Gospel of John: A Commentary (Grand Rapids, MI: Eerdmans, 2012), 132.

CHAPTER 12: JESUS WITH THE DEAD

Epigraph: Frederick Buechner, *Beyond Words: Daily Readings in the ABC's of Faith* (New York: HarperCollins, 2004), 122.

1. James R. Edwards, *The Gospel According to Luke*, The Pillar New Testament Commentary (Grand Rapids, MI: Eerdmans, 2015), 213.
2. R. C. H. Lenski, *The Interpretation of St. Luke's Gospel* (Minneapolis: Augsburg Publishing House, 1961), 400.
3. David E. Garland, *The NIV Application Commentary: Mark* (Grand Rapids, MI: Zondervan, 1996), 225.
4. Ibid., 222.
5. Gary M. Burge, *The NIV Application Commentary: John* (Grand Rapids, MI: Zondervan, 2000), 318.
6. Garland, *Mark*, 226.

CHAPTER 13: JESUS WITH THE OUTCAST

Epigraph: Brennan Manning, *The Ragamuffin Gospel* (Colorado Springs: Multnomah Books, 2015), 8.

CHAPTER 14: JESUS WITH THE RULE FOLLOWERS

Epigraph: Michael Horton, *Christless Christianity* (Grand Rapids, MI: Baker Books, 2008), 15–16.

1. David E. Garland, *The NIV Application Commentary: Mark* (Grand Rapids, MI: Zondervan, 1996), 395.
2. R. C. H. Lenski, *The Interpretation of St. Mark's Gospel* (Minneapolis: Augsburg Publishing House, 1961), 436.
3. R. Alan Cole, "Mark," in *New Bible Commentary: 21st Century Edition*, ed. D. A. Carson et al., 4th ed. (Downers Grove, IL: InterVarsity Press, 1994), 962.
4. Gustaf Wingren, *Luther on Vocation* (Eugene, OR: Wipf and Stock, 2004), 10.

CHAPTER 15: JESUS WITH THOSE WHO HATED HIM

Epigraph: Martin Luther King, Jr., quoted in Clayborne Carson and Peter Holloran, eds., *A Knock at Midnight: Inspiration from the Great Sermons of Reverend Martin Luther King, Jr.* (New York: Warner Books, 2000), 53–54.

1. Walter A. Elwell and Barry J. Beitzel, "Pharisees," in *Baker Encyclopedia of the Bible* (Grand Rapids, MI: Baker Books, 1988), 1672.
2. Ibid.
3. R. C. H. Lenski, *The Interpretation of St. Luke's Gospel* (Minneapolis: Augsburg Publishing House, 1961), 259.
4. Ibid., 260.

CHAPTER 16: JESUS WITH HIS BETRAYER

Epigraph: Agatha Christie, *The Mirror Crack'd from Side to Side* (New York: HarperCollins, 2016), 134.
1. Edward A. Engelbrecht, ed., *The Lutheran Study Bible* (St. Louis, MO: Concordia Publishing House, 2009), 1808.
2. Ibid., 1809.
3. R. C. H. Lenski, *The Interpretation of St. Luke's Gospel* (Minneapolis: Augsburg Publishing House, 1961), 1079–80.
4. Engelbrecht, *The Lutheran Study Bible*, 1766.

CHAPTER 17: JESUS WITH YOU

1. James K. A. Smith, *On the Road with Saint Augustine: A Real-World Spirituality for Restless Hearts* (Grand Rapids, MI: Brazos Press, 2019), 49.
2. Frederick Dale Bruner, *The Gospel of John: A Commentary* (Grand Rapids, MI: Eerdmans, 2012), 888.
3. Colin G. Kruse, *John: An Introduction and Commentary*, vol. 4, Tyndale New Testament Commentaries (Downers Grove, IL: InterVarsity Press, 2003), 315.